Praise for
Rituals Roadmap

"Erica's done it again! She's now paired her knack for human engagement with healthy workplace rituals to make everyone's days that much brighter! *Rituals Roadmap* is brimming with important science and inspiring stories of real people's rituals at work. Teaching us how to turn ordinary routines into workplace magic, this is the perfect book for these extraordinary times."

—KATIE COURIC
journalist and bestselling author

"Erica Keswin knows a lot about how to make routines and relationships more meaningful. In this book, she shows that rituals aren't just for family holiday gatherings—they can be useful at work too."

—ADAM GRANT
New York Times bestselling author of *Originals* and
Give and Take, and host of the TED podcast *WorkLife*

"Erica Keswin's latest book, *Rituals Roadmap*, couldn't have come at a better time. Filled with firsthand stories from some of the biggest companies in the world, fascinating science, and her very human voice, Keswin makes a convincing business case for rituals as the tools of the human workplace. Whether you're an entrepreneur, a leader, or looking for your next breakthrough idea, harnessing the power of rituals is something we can all do, all the time. This is an important book."

—DORIE CLARK
author of *Reinventing You* and executive education faculty,
Duke University Fuqua School of Business

"Erica Keswin's first book, *Bring Your Human to Work*, changed the way we think about workplace culture. The Female Quotient has been fortunate to partner with Erica many times (and bond over lots of spaghetti dinners in the Equality Lounge!), and I am constantly impressed by her depth as a speaker, dot-connector, and advocate for diversity and inclusion. Her second book, *Rituals Roadmap*, is delightful and insightful. Blending science and firsthand stories, it's a masterclass in deepening employee engagement and drawing power from everyday routines. Highly recommended reading, even—or especially—for the most seasoned leaders!"

—SHELLEY ZALIS
founder and CEO Female Quotient

"In *Rituals Roadmap*, Erica Keswin shows how rituals boost productivity by creating psychological safety and connecting us to a purpose. It's a message we all need now more than ever, and for anyone looking to bring their workforce together during tough times, *Rituals Roadmap* is an essential guide."

—CHARLES DUHIGG
author of bestsellers *The Power of Habit*
and *Smarter Faster Better*

"Chock-full of easy-to-implement and creative examples, *Rituals Roadmap* is an enlightening guide to help managers and individuals make work more special."

—LIZ FOSSLIEN and MOLLIE WEST DUFFY
Wall Street Journal bestselling coauthors
of *No Hard Feelings: The Secret Power*
of Embracing Emotions at Work.

"So, it's not just me who loves Taco Tuesday and Wine Wednesday? Erica Keswin's *Rituals Roadmap* showcases how important rituals are—at work and in our daily lives. I loved reading the case studies and diving into the science behind why repeat practices are so important in workplaces and communities. Kudos to Erica on another great book—practical, enjoyable, and will help you sweat the small stuff . . . but in the best way possible."

—RANDI ZUCKERBERG
New York Times bestselling author of
Pick Three and *Dot Complicated*

"In unsettling and changing times, humans search for meaningful connection and a sense of belonging. In *Rituals Roadmap*, Erica Keswin advises leaders to be attentive to those yearnings and offers the perfect leadership response—the magic of rituals. And magic it is. Erica highlights a simple but profound truth: intentional practices and traditions can have astounding impacts on the engagement, productivity, retention, and performance of your teams. As leaders, we need to become fluent in creating and facilitating touchpoint experiences to amplify important moments, highlight key transitions, remind us who we are, who we aspire to be, and where we can return for comfort when times get tough. If you're interested in living your organizational values OUT LOUD, then *Rituals Roadmap* is a great addition to your modern leadership philosophy."

—CY WAKEMAN
New York Times bestselling author, *No Ego*

"*Rituals Roadmap* makes it clear that rituals are one of the most vital tools we have for managing our well-being at work and at home. Through storytelling and research, Keswin illustrates the powerful ways rituals can help people and organizations address the uncertainty we all face. Daily rituals build a positive mind-set, reduce anxiety, and drive us to action—they are a celebration that involves our emotions and our full attention. At the end of this book, you will be equipped and inspired to create your own rituals roadmap!"

—JEN FISHER
chief well-being officer, Deloitte

"Erica Keswin's new book *Rituals Roadmap* has arrived at precisely the perfect moment in time. In an era of widespread disruption and change, Erica shows us exactly why rituals are about more than just staying personally grounded and connected to a company's mission. *Rituals Roadmap* finds an inspiring and engaging balance between personal stories and company case studies to demonstrate the value of cultures of true diversity. This book is smart, accessible, and an undeniably bright moment in an otherwise dark time. I urge every leader to dive into its pages with an open mind and a notepad at the ready—I promise it will yield insightful and business-saving strategies for weathering these difficult times!"

—JENNIFER BROWN
author, *How to Be an Inclusive Leader*

RITUALS
ROADMAP

The Human Way to Transform Everyday Routines into Workplace Magic

Erica Keswin

New York   Chicago   San Francisco   Athens   London   Madrid
Mexico City   Milan   New Delhi   Singapore   Sydney   Toronto

1 2 3 4 5 6 7 8 9   LCR   26 25 24 23 22 21

ISBN   978-1-260-46189-3
MHID   1-260-46189-0

e-ISBN   978-1-260-46190-9
e-MHID   1-260-46190-4

Library of Congress Cataloging-in-Publication Data

Names: Keswin, Erica, author.
Title: Rituals roadmap : the human way to transform everyday routines
    into workplace magic / Erica Keswin.
Description: New York : McGraw Hill Education, [2021] | Includes
    bibliographical references and index.
Identifiers: LCCN 2020032546 (print) | LCCN 2020032547 (ebook) |
    ISBN 9781260461893 (hardback) | ISBN 9781260461909 (ebook)
Subjects: LCSH: Corporate culture. | Employee motivation. | Work
    environment. | Manners and customs. | Quality of work life.
Classification: LCC HD58.7 .K464566 2021 (print) | LCC HD58.7
    (ebook) | DDC 658.3—dc23
LC record available at https://lccn.loc.gov/2020032546
LC ebook record available at https://lccn.loc.gov/2020032547

McGraw Hill books are available at special quantity discounts to use as premiums and sales promotions or for use in corporate training programs. To contact a representative, please visit the Contact Us pages at www.mhprofessional.com.

CONTENTS

PREFACE
Rituals During COVID-19

It was the evening of May 18th. I had been quarantined in Connecticut for two months and five days with my family. My daughter Julia and I had returned to New York City for one night to pick up some spring clothes.

I was standing in my office, which overlooks West End Avenue, when the clock struck 7:00 p.m. Like clockwork, people of all ages opened their windows, banged pots and pans, and shouted at the top of their lungs. Julia and I joined in as I caught the eye of someone in the building across the street, and we both smiled.

Even in the face of so much death and uncertainty, this ritual transformed my day—and the day of so many others—into magic. But how?

First, we felt a strong sense of belonging and like we were part of the collective. We're New Yorkers, after all. At 7:00 p.m., we could hear it, see it, and feel it. We also felt a sense of purpose. At 7:00 p.m., we had one job—to pause and thank the healthcare workers for putting themselves at risk to save us. We cheered them on to keep on going so that together we could win the war on this pandemic.

In those moments, Julia and I were transported out of our own lives and connected to something bigger. I don't think I will ever think about 7:00 p.m. the same way again. That's the magic of rituals.

Six weeks prior, on March 30th, I had turned in the manuscript for this book, *Rituals Roadmap*, to my editor at McGraw Hill. I had been quarantined with my family for a little over two weeks. I wondered what it would all mean for my book as the world had been turned upside down overnight. As I reached out to clients, leaders at companies of all sizes, friends, and family to connect about what had quickly become our "new normal," people started talking to me about how they were turning to their rituals to support themselves and each other during these uncertain times. And, I realized, so was I.

While some of the companies in this book have gone through changes to their businesses in the months since the manuscript was completed and some of the numbers have changed, the concepts and the ideas you are about to explore are more relevant than ever. As the pandemic continued, and we remained quarantined into June, I decided to add a new chapter to the book called "Rituals in Turbulent Times" to include as an addendum. In this new chapter, I highlight companies that have maintained their rituals in the face of COVID-19, or created new ones. I will also share some important lessons that we can carry with us into a post-COVID world.

Whether employees work remotely, in an office, or somewhere in between, I'm more convinced than ever that even the simplest of rituals are the human way to transform everyday routines into workplace—even worldwide—magic. And while I can't know what the state of the world will be in January 2021 when this book hits the shelves, I can confidently say that as of this day in June of 2020, as I write this new preface, our world has never needed that magic more.

DON'T STOP BELIEVIN'

A Business Case for Rituals

When I was doing the research for my first book, *Bring Your Human to Work*, I came across a research study that changed my life.

Professor Kevin Kniffin, an organizational psychologist at Cornell University, wanted to understand what made some teams more productive than others. His father was a firefighter, so that's who he studied—those were his people. His research found that the firefighters most devoted to the long-standing tradition of making and sharing the firehouse meal, usually something cozy like spaghetti and meatballs, outperformed those who didn't. And it was the relationships they formed and strengthened around the table that made all the difference. And when we're talking about firefighters' "performance," remember, we're talking about saving lives.[1]

I could hardly believe it. A plate of pasta is literally a matter of life and death!

I was so intrigued by this research, I had to learn more. I reached out to Professor Kniffin, interviewed firefighters, and it wasn't long before I became a true believer. Eventually I even started my own business, the Spaghetti Project, paying homage to the firefighters' classic meal. I created an intentional, communal ritual for companies and organizations because, well, left to our own devices (excuse the cheesy pun), it was clear to me that we're just not connecting. I took it upon myself to make connections happen by sitting down with people and letting the oxytocin—our feel-good hormone—flow.

Every month for the past four years, I've been hosting a Spaghetti Project for a group of people with a common interest. Sometimes we'll meet in an office, sometimes in a coffee shop, and sometimes in a living room. What I've found is that good things happen when people connect. And while spaghetti and meatballs are definitely conversation starters, more and more I've realized it's the ritual of it all that really counts.

It's the ritual that transforms a plate of pasta into lifesaving magic.

So, what exactly *is* a ritual? Is every meal a ritual?

Not really.

So, then, what's the difference between a habit, a routine, a ritual, and a rule?

These are some of the questions I've been exploring, and I'm excited to share some of the answers with you in this book.

We tend to think of rituals as things we do to punctuate important life experiences—like baby showers, bat mitzvahs, weddings, and funerals. We also know that rituals are often repeated, like saying grace at a meal or meditating in the morning. But rituals don't need to be reserved for big milestones, and just doing something again and again does not a ritual make. The transformational power of rituals lies in *both* our intention and how these activities make us feel. As a group of scholars you'll meet soon put it, rituals are rituals because they "mean something to the people enacting them."[2]

Rituals are purposeful. Rituals are personal.

Because rituals are inherently personal, the very idea of rituals at work might strike you as odd. Allow me to explain. We know there are lots of things we do again and again at work (ad infinitum even), but we don't normally associate these things with anything remotely magical. Take meetings, for instance. We all have meetings every single Monday (and Tuesday, and Wednesday and . . . you get the picture), but they don't usually feel like something we're doing with much intention. How about a company happy hour? Maybe that's a ritual? For some, perhaps, while for others it's simply a chore. How about your team's lunchtime gatherings? Do they mean something to the group, or is it just something that you do? What about the company holiday party? Orientation? Milestones? Awards and recognition? Promotions, feedback, end-of-day reflections?

Remember smoke breaks? Of course you don't. Well, when people used to step outside for a cigarette, it was very ritual-ized—it happened at a certain time, a certain place, and with a certain crew. Smoking is bad for our health, obviously, but lone-liness is just as bad as smoking 15 cigarettes a day.[3] Stepping out for a smoke was a ritual that created a deeply personal feeling of belonging. What have we done to replace it? I'm concerned that we haven't done enough to help us feel like we're part of something, something bigger than ourselves, more meaningful than our Instagram feed or our list of to-dos.

As you read on, consider your own life at work and what calls out to you as something you do that gives you a sense of purpose—whether it's a collective experience or something you do personally. What makes *you* feel like you belong? And think about this nugget of wisdom from Maria Popova, founder of the popular website *Brain Pickings*: "though very different in practice, routine and ritual seem to be two sides of the same coin . . . the structure of routine comforts us, and the special-ness of ritual vitalizes us."[4]

Vitalizes? *Really*? Can rituals really vitalize us?

You bet they can. Rituals are that powerful.

Rituals are—in a word—magic.

The Science Behind the Magic of Rituals

Imagine being ushered into a room set up with a karaoke machine. An experimenter hands you the mic and says, "Sing into this microphone. The lyrics will appear across the bottom of the screen." You'll probably feel ridiculous as you awkwardly sing along to none other than Journey's famous anthem, one of the most downloaded songs in iTunes history, "Don't Stop Believin'." To make matters weirder, a stranger—the experimenter—sits in front of you and watches. Your face is hot, your voice shakes. Why are you doing this? You actually *don't* believe it!

Afterward, you receive a score. You get five dollars if you are deemed "accurate."

In this study, published by an esteemed group of Ivy League organizational psychologists in 2016, researchers concluded that rituals actually "improve performance in public and private performance domains by decreasing anxiety."[5] They discovered this by giving two groups of people the same stressful task—singing in public—but under two different conditions. Before this group of 85 students was led into their private singing chamber, they were split into two groups.

Each person in the first group was told to perform a ritual—"Draw a picture of how you are feeling right now. Sprinkle salt on your drawing. Count to five out loud. Crinkle up your paper. Throw your paper in the trash."

Everyone in the second group was told to sit quietly for one minute.

Guess who sang more accurately and won more money?

Yep. The ritual group was more accurate (and five dollars richer). Why? Because, the researchers believe, they were less anxious.

To further back their data, they also tracked the singers' heart rates. While everyone's heart rate spiked when told they would have to sing in front of a stranger, the ritual group had an easier time bringing their heart rates back to normal, compared to those instructed merely to "calm down."

In another version of the study, performing a ritual boosted math performance.[6] Clearly, something important is happening with even the simplest of rituals. So what exactly is a "ritual" from a scientific standpoint, and how is it defined?

The authors of the aforementioned study define ritual as "a predefined sequence of symbolic actions, often characterized by formality and repetition that lacks direct instrumental purpose."[7] What does it mean for something to "lack instrumental purpose?" Put simply, as much as rituals ease our anxiety and up our game, rituals don't always make much sense. Unlike a routine, which is conducted with the goal of preparing for something, a ritual is performed without the specific goal of preparation in mind. Researchers in the Ivy League study illustrate the distinction with athletic warm-ups, explaining that, "each step in the routine is functionally linked to preparing an athlete to perform at their best (e.g., stretching muscles to improve flexibility); in contrast, a warm-up ritual may involve some of same steps with the same goal, but is composed of steps that are not logically necessary for preparation—such as bouncing a basketball exactly three times or conducting certain steps in a particular fixed sequence. . . . To be considered a ritual, at least some—though not necessarily all—of the constituent behaviors must be noninstrumental.[8]"

Another example of this distinction is an artist or a surgeon preparing her tools. You can't very well paint or perform surgery without your brushes and scalpels. Whether or not tool preparation is a ritualized activity depends on if it is "composed of steps that are not logically necessary," meaning the tools are laid out in a particular order—smallest to largest, for instance—with a certain rhythm, which induces a state of mind, which is carried over into the art, or the healing.[9]

This is what makes rituals kind of magical. Rituals work, but they also play. And we could all use more of that!

The Business Case for Rituals at Work

Technology has changed absolutely everything about the world of work as we know it. We're able to work anywhere, anytime. We're abandoning the traditional office, we're transient, and we're in a constant state of "on duty," battling our inbox and notifications, trying to hang on to our most valuable asset—our attention. It's the Wild West! We feel like this technology has been around forever, but the first iPhone was released in 2007, so as I'm writing this very sentence, the most important invention that changed everything about our lives is just 13 years old, a very young teenager. Need I say more?

In the midst of all this hyper-connection, as former surgeon general, Dr. Vivek Murthy, has been telling us, one of the biggest health risks facing our country is—no, not smoking, not secondhand smoke, and not even sitting, but rather—loneliness and isolation.

In other words, as I mentioned earlier, left to our own devices, we're just not connecting. And it's hurting us. And our businesses. Our engagement levels are abysmally low. Gallup found that in 2019, "based on a random sample of 4,700 full- and part-time U.S. employees working for an employer from January to August 2019," 35 percent of employees are engaged.[10] Just 35 out of 100 workers are into what they're doing! And the crazy thing is that's a *record high* since they started tracking in 2000. Of course we want that percentage to be so much higher. That's why in my first book, I made a case for the human workplace, which really boils down to the fact that honoring relationships leads to more engagement. Bringing our human to work is not just good for people, but great for business, and just might change the world.

And here's the thing: rituals, I've found, are the tools of the human workplace. In fact, they are elemental to our lives. According to scholars across disciplines, rituals are a "psychologically prepared, culturally inherited, behavioral trademark of our species."[11] Scientists say that one of the reasons we humans love rituals is to "maintain group cohesion."[12] In this world of disparate disconnection, rituals come to the rescue.

But don't worry. This is not some snake-oil sales pitch. In fact, there's nothing to buy. Not only are rituals just something humans do, they're also great for the bottom line because most don't cost a penny. The investment required to blend rituals into our work life is psychological, emotional, and strategic, but it's not necessarily financial. The cost of most rituals is minimal, but their value is priceless. And the impact is significant: more connection (improved cooperation, social cohesion, and perceived social support),[13] higher productivity (through regulation of top-down and bottom-up psychosocial processing in our brains),[14] better engagement, and a decrease in anxiety and stress. In other words, a positive work culture.

According to researchers Emma Seppälä (faculty director of the Women's Leadership Program at the Yale School of Management and science director of Stanford University's Center for Compassion and Altruism Research and Education) and Kim Cameron (William Russell Kelly Professor of Management and Organizations at the Ross School of Business at the University of Michigan and the author of *Positive Leadership* and *Practicing Positive Leadership*), in a positive, engaged workforce "people get sick less often, recover twice as fast from surgery, experience less depression, learn faster and remember longer, tolerate pain and discomfort better, display more mental acuity, and perform better on the job."[15] Plus, for those with poor social relationships, their probability of dying early is 70 percent higher than those with stronger connections. This might sound dramatic, but as a point of comparison, Sarah Pressman, an associate professor of psychological science at the University of California, Irvine, found that "toxic, stress-filled workplaces affect social relationships and, consequently, life expectancy."[16]

In case this all sounds expensive, the opposite is actually true. Seppälä and Cameron maintain that having a "positive work culture" is incredibly cost-effective. "The American Psychological Association estimates that more than $500 billion is siphoned off from the U.S. economy because of workplace stress, and 550 million workdays are lost each year due to stress on the job." Furthermore, "Sixty percent to 80 percent of workplace accidents are attributed to stress, and it's estimated that more than 80 percent of doctor visits are due to stress. Workplace stress has been linked to health problems ranging from metabolic syndrome to cardiovascular disease and mortality."[17]

From a bottom-line point of view, the value of rituals at work is without question.

But maybe even with all these bottom-line numbers about engagement and culture, you still think rituals are a little "soft." You're just not convinced that rituals can really move the needle on the employee experience. I accept your challenge. I invite you to think of a time when you were in a highly ritualized space but didn't know the rules, when you perhaps blushed with embarrassment and discomfort. Visiting a friend's church, or, say, your first fancy, confusing, multi-fork dinner? A leader at Twitter shared a story with me about the time she arrived at her prestigious business school, and somehow everyone else had gotten the memo that they were supposed to applaud at specific times. She felt so lost and out-of-sync that she actually felt like leaving the program.

Is this how we'd ever want people on our teams to feel? Awkward, out of step, afraid of doing the wrong thing, dying to get out of there?

Especially on their first day on the job?

Of course not. It's widely accepted that friendship[18] and personal connections[19] are necessary ingredients for a successful workplace. Don't we want our new employees to feel like they're in the right place instead of like a hockey player at a cotillion?

And the same goes for people of color, women, and LGBTQIA+ folks. Study after study show that in order for people to be their best, most engaged selves at work, they need to feel connected—to their colleagues, to the company mission, and to themselves.

This is also true for our remote workers, whose numbers have increased more than 159 percent between 2005 and 2017, (and of course skyrocketed through the roof because of COVID-19[20]). We don't want them to feel out of step. And remote working may well be here to stay.

On May 21, 2020, Mark Zuckerberg, Facebook's chief executive, told workers during a staff meeting that was live-streamed on his Facebook page that within a decade, as many as half of the company's more than 48,000 employees would work from home.

"It's clear that COVID has changed a lot about our lives, and that certainly includes the way that most of us work," Zuckerberg said. "Coming out of this period, I expect that remote work is going to be a growing trend, as well."[21] Twitter and Square, the online payment giant, are both allowing employees to work from home indefinitely.

Get ready for big changes. Rituals can work their magic from the office, at home, and everywhere in between.

In this next section, I'll share a simple formula I've created that captures the power of rituals at work and serves as a guide to help us create rituals in our own organizations. I hope you'll find it helpful.

The Three P's of Rituals: Psychological Safety + Purpose = Performance

As I've spent the last year studying the science and stories of workplace rituals, I've come to see that there is a simple equation at work. I've realized that rituals are so impactful because they harness two of the core elements every human needs to succeed: psychological safety (or a sense of belonging) and purpose. When we feel psychologically safe and connected to a purpose, like the firefighters around a table, our performance improves. This is what I call the Three P's of rituals.

Psychological Safety

According to Harvard Business School professor Amy Edmondson "[P]sychological safety is a crucial source of value creation in organizations operating in a complex, changing environment."[22] Sharing rituals at work is the perfect way to help us feel included, and thus safe from the threat of social exclusion. Edmondson found that study after study from around the world linked psychological safety to worker engagement,[23] which, as I described earlier, is very good for business.

I spoke with Daisy Auger-Dominguez, a workplace strategist who designs "Inclusive & Equitable Workplace & Social Impact Strategies." She told me about a brilliant ritual she uses to create psychological safety with her client teams. "Whenever I've taken over a new team or function, I have everyone participate in 'manager integration exercises,'" wherein she encourages people to consider the impression she (or any manager) leaves on a group. She explains, "My favorite is where I come together with my direct reports, and then I leave the room so that they can answer three questions: (1) What do we know about Daisy? (2) What do we wish we knew about Daisy? (3) What do we wish Daisy would know about us? I then come back to the group, review the answers, which are not attributed to anyone in particular unless they want to, and add, complement, etc. It's a great trust-building exercise that requires a huge level of transparency and vulnerability." This ritual shows psychological safety in action.[24]

A lack of psychological safety, as Auger-Dominguez explains, "reduces the chances of a free exchange of ideas necessary for innovation and high performance. The challenge is that we can often make others feel excluded or at risk of rejection without realizing it." So her manager integration ritual is the perfect remedy to accidentally excluding people.

A study by Catalyst, a preeminent global nonprofit helping women advance in the workplace, talks about the toll that an "emotional tax" can have on employees. What's an emotional tax? We know it when we feel it: "At work, you feel a constant need to protect against what others might say or do, whether they intend to exclude you or not. Throughout the day, you might find yourself bracing for insults, avoiding social interactions and places, or adjusting your appearance to protect against hurtful situations. Put simply, you live each day in a constant state of being 'on guard.' "[25]

We can all relate to this feeling, for "a majority of women and men across racial and ethnic groups—58 percent—report being highly on guard" at work.[26]

Rituals help ensure that we're *all* included.

An overwhelming body of research shows that diversity, inclusion, and belonging are not just nice-to-haves for the bottom line. They're crucial. For example, a recent study from the Boston Consulting Group found that diverse companies generate 19 percent more revenue compared to companies with below-average diversity scores.[27] And in a 2018 report, McKinsey found that "companies in the top quartile for gender diversity on their executive teams were 21 percent more likely to experience above-average profitability than companies in the fourth quartile. . . . For ethnic and cultural diversity, the 2017 finding was a 33 percent likelihood of outperformance."[28] These numbers don't lie. Rituals are the tools to help accelerate that sense of belonging, gathering *all kinds* of people together. True psychological safety has never mattered more.

Purpose

In an oft-quoted 2019 Gallup study on purpose in the workplace, the author writes, "Astute leaders increasingly understand the effect purpose has on business outcomes. But purpose can't be limited to just a slogan. To advance, inspire and unite a company, purpose must be actualized in the day-to-day work."[29]

What better way to tie employees directly to a company's purpose than through rituals? The Gallup author mentions rituals specifically as part of a corporate communication program that should be audited annually.

Larry Fink is the influential CEO of Black Rock Financial who caused quite a stir with his 2019 letter to CEOs when he wrote, "Purpose is not the sole pursuit of profits but the animating force for achieving them."[30] What a concept, huh? What would it be like to live in a world where profit was not the number one purpose for companies to exist?

One of the conversations I have the most with leaders of companies around the world is about the importance of values. I often tell people that they have to get their values off the walls and into the halls for their purpose to come to life. This is one of those evergreen concepts that everyone thinks they've got covered. I can't tell you the number of leaders of major Fortune 500 companies who say to me, "Oh, yes, of course we have values," but then can't tell me what they are. Values won't help anyone unless they're authentic and functional and memorable.

Follow these two steps to make sure you have functional values:

Step one: Develop a set of values that everyone in the company can recite. Three to five is a good number.

Step two: Use rituals to tie people to your values. According to social psychologist Heidi Grant, rituals help people value their experience more deeply.[31]

Voilà!

In a world where "73 percent of employees who say they work at a 'purpose-driven' company are engaged, compared to just 23 percent of those who don't,"[32] we can't afford to let employees flit about purposelessly. Rituals are here to help ground and guide.

Performance

When we put psychological safety and purpose together, what do we get? Better performance, that's what.

Firefighters save more lives when they eat together. A study at Google found that rituals were the key to more effective teams.[33] What will you and your company do when you take a seat around your table?

As Paolo Guenzi writes in his *Harvard Business Review* article, "If performance is struggling at your company, maybe a bit more ritual can deliver that sense of shared identity, stakeholder commitment, emotional energy, and productive behavior that you're looking for."[34] In a study on preperformance rituals, researchers in Australia found that ten-pin bowlers' performance improved 29 percent when they participated in a preperformance ritual (or "PPR") prior to competing. They found that "Using the personalized PPR produced adaptive and relevant, task-focused attention."[35] In an experiment at the University of Toronto, researchers found that subjects participating in arbitrary ritual-novel actions before an executive function task reduced their neural response to performance error. In other words, "ritual guides goal-directed performance by regulating the brain's response to personal failure."[36]

The Three P's are just a way of pointing out what rituals do for us—they help us feel connected in an increasingly disconnected world. Rituals are the tools of the human workplace.

Creating Your Own Rituals Roadmap

It's late afternoon at one of the most prestigious newsrooms in the world, the *New York Times*. The noise of concentration—phones ringing, conversation swirling, keyboards clicking—fills the room as reporters, photographers, and editors deliver today's news. At 4 p.m. they hear something in the distance. They pause. A whirring sound comes closer. They look up from their work, then at each other.

It's the afternoon snack cart. Break time!

In one giant, collective exhale, the group stretches its legs, finishes phone calls, and stands up. Everyone presses "save" on open documents and walks over to the cart to grab a coffee, a roll, a protein bar, and chat with their colleagues and friends. They gossip, share their personal updates, commiserate, and make plans. After 10 or 15 minutes, they dutifully return to their desks to tell the world's stories, refreshed.

This 4 p.m. break in the routine happens every day. Until . . . the day the snack cart stops coming. The newspaper has done some restructuring and changes have been made.

Sadly, and abruptly, the snack cart days came to an end.

Even though the folks in the newsroom could still walk down the hall to the vending machine or even run downstairs for a cup of coffee, they were crestfallen. Mind you, these are not hourly workers with a foreman watching over them, timing their bathroom visits. They can take a break whenever they need one. So why did the loss of the snack cart hit them so hard?

The answer is that the snack cart grew to be more than just caffeine and calories on wheels. It was a ritual. And like all rituals, it was loved for reasons beyond the rational, and it was sorely missed when it was gone.

Rituals are something we do—getting a cup of coffee—but so much more than an activity (remember the artist and surgeon laying out their tools?). They help us connect to a very important purpose—caffeine!—and move us beyond the practical. We can try to create or design rituals out of the blue, but we so often have really powerful rituals already at work, and all we need to do is recognize them. Organizational psychologist Melissa Gratias defines ritual simply as "part of our day-to-day activities that lead to desired outcomes."[37] Rituals change us and conjure lifelong commitments and community out of a slice of cake or a dollar bill under a pillow. And that's just in our personal lives. Moreover, if you've ever been to church, jury duty, or a parade, you've entered a truly ritual-rich zone filled with activities meant to achieve a certain outcome. If you're a human being, you live in ritual territory.

At DoSomething, a not-for-profit that connects millennials with meaningful volunteer opportunities, they pass a stuffed penguin around as part of their weekly all-hands meeting for no good reason other than as a way of celebrating individuals and honoring relationships. While CEO Aria Finger insists this fun, totally DoSomething ritual is "enduring," its origin was a pretty random event. An employee had a penguin on his desk and started giving it to people. That's it! While that person, in fact, is no longer with the company, the ritual sure is. And the employee's legacy has been passed down like a Thanksgiving tradition.

See what I mean? Rituals are magical because they don't have to make any sense and yet are vital to people coming together collectively and creatively—they're the glue that keeps us together. From a business point of view, what could be better than employees feeling as strongly about a shared experience at work as they do about whether or not the mashed potatoes have lumps or no lumps?

Rituals are a surefire way to help people connect.

Reading about the science and the stories of rituals at work, you, too, will learn how to be on the lookout for ritual-rich opportunities in your own workplace—from the top down, from the bottom up, and from the inside out. Because when it comes to rituals, it's the little things. As SYPartners' principal Joshua-Michéle Ross puts it, "It's about redesigning the way people interact from an atomic level."[38] It can be challenging for big-picture visionaries to keep an eye out for granular opportunities that might be so obvious they're hard to see, but that's where a lot of our rituals happen. After spending two years talking to people about rituals, I'm more convinced than ever that it's the ordinary, everyday things that help us feel connected. In fact, it's our routines that we can turn into magic.

When I began my interview process, I asked people all kinds of questions about rituals. After several rounds of honing my questions, I discovered the prompt that inspired the best, most detailed stories about rituals at work: *What do you and your employees do that makes you feel the most "KIND/ Chipotle/LinkedIn"-ish or the most like an employee of your organization? In other words, what makes you feel most like you belong to this unique group of human beings?*

When I asked this question of Joey Zwillinger, the cofounder of Allbirds, "the world's most comfortable shoe," I could not have predicted his cool answer. "I would say that employees feel most like Allbirds employees when they take their shift sitting at reception. People sign up every quarter to do one or two shifts at reception—including [his cofounder] Tim and myself. We don't have a full-time receptionist so people take turns. We call it rotating reception. . . . Reception can feel like a job that's below people. And we want to make sure that everyone understands that that's not the way we think."

These answers always pointed to truly original, very effective, atom-level events and interactions that *make people feel like they belong to the company they work for.* So this is a great place to start as you create your own roadmap, identifying rituals at your company.

This is not rocket science. Humans are better off when they do things that connect them to each other and to their purpose. And when companies support them, everyone wins.

It might seem far-fetched, but it's often the simplest, homespun rituals that help us thread the needle, move the dial, or kick some butt on our loftiest, most aspirational goals at work.

How This Book Is Structured

The rituals roadmap that follows traces the employee lifecycle from the first day to the last and everything in between, as well as a day-in-the-life of employees today—meetings, eatings, and taking breaks. As you follow along, each chapter is dedicated to a specific stop on the workplace roadmap where rituals can thrive.

At the end of every chapter of our rituals roadmap, I invite you to pause to see how you can apply the lessons learned and to consider opportunities for rituals in your organization and in your life. This is what I call a Yield for Rituals section—an opportunity to slow down and take stock before moving ahead. Just like on any road, signs tell us when to stop, go, slow down, watch for deer crossing, and yield. And so, on our rituals road trip, we'll take a minute after each chapter to pause, so you can think about how to make each ritual work for you.

Finally, in Chapter 10, I invite you to design your very own rituals roadmap, using everything that you've learned on our journey together. All maps have a key, denoting landmarks and directions. This final chapter is the key to our rituals road-map that will help you make the leap into becoming a rituals rockstar.

So, let's begin our journey. I hope to make a believer out of you.

The authors of the study, "Don't Stop Believin'" are total rockstars!

CHAPTER ONE

ALL ABOARD

Rituals for Recruiting, Hiring, and Onboarding

Our first stop on the rituals roadmap is—where else?—getting people on board. And in case you haven't heard, the race for talent is on. As recently as 2019, across the entire labor market, there were 1.4 million more jobs than unemployed people, according to the Job Openings and Labor Turnover Survey.[1] And according to *Industry Week*, "13 STEM jobs were posted online for each unemployed STEM worker in 2016. That translates to 3 million more jobs than job seekers."[2] Of course once COVID-19 hit, and more than 40 million Americans lost their jobs from March to May alone,[3] these numbers changed, but the principles are evergreen. Because top candidates have their pick of top jobs (which 43 percent of millennials indicated they may well leave within two years,[4] costing companies up to two times that person's salary,[5]) businesses have no choice but to evolve. After all, according to the Faas Foundation and Mental Health America, "a full 71 percent of employees are thinking about—or actively looking—for new jobs."[6] So evolving is a must, indeed.

What does evolution at work look like?

It looks less like the world of the show *The Office*, with Michael Scott at the top of a ridiculous hierarchy, and more like the warm, welcoming Central Perk community hub of *Friends*. Though, interestingly, both megahit shows are great examples of how groups of people are tied together through rituals. People need to get their quest for meaning with a capital *M* fulfilled somehow, and with church and synagogue attendance down 12 percent since 2009,[7] what better way to find fulfillment than at work, where we spend a majority of our lives? Not exactly the solution I would have guessed, but it's true.

The way I see it, evolving to be a more human workplace means curating communities inside of work, supporting people's need to have a life outside of work, and inviting people's whole selves to work. This is not an easy task, but throughout the tenure of our employees, rituals can help us evolve. And while I would never want to say that any one step along the path is more important than another, I will say getting it right from the beginning impacts everything else down the line.

Something I think about a lot and, in fact, referenced in *Bring Your Human to Work*, was some advice from the British pediatrician Dr. Penelope Leach that I followed back when my three kids were all under the age of five. "Start the way you mean to go on." In other words, if you want to raise a well-mannered teen, make sure your toddler knows not to throw her Cheerios on the floor. A beginning isn't just another random moment in time. The beginning sets the tone for everything that follows. Kickoff rituals have a lot of power.

Have you ever seen the New Zealand All Blacks rugby team begin a match? It's one of the most impressive things I've ever witnessed. Before the All Blacks begin, they perform what's called the Haka, a traditional Māori dance that is the very embodiment of ferocity and strength. Together, they move across the field, rhythmically chanting, slapping their bodies, sticking out their tongues, and bulging their eyes. The other team stands there on the field, spellbound and awestruck. In one video, their French opponents actually started holding hands. I don't blame them. The Haka is a pure expression of a group's prowess. Who wouldn't want to be a part of that group? Unsurprisingly, as of March 2020, in World Cups, they've scored the most points of all time (2,552), won the most matches (56, an 88 percent win percentage), and are tied with South Africa for most Rugby World Cup wins.[8] According to author and business professor Paolo Guenzi in a *Harvard Business Review* article, the All Blacks' Haka dance "expresses the team's pride in their heritage and teammates." What's more, "Neuroscientific research shows that rituals like the Haka trigger feelings of connectivity, timelessness, and meaning, which stimulate mental flow states. These, in turn, reduce anxiety and increase energy and focus."[9] This shared sense of pride and connectivity makes all the difference in their performance as a team.

Our work rituals might not be as passionate or physical as a Haka dance, and that's OK. The point is that when we throw ourselves into whatever we do, we can get our blood moving and feel more connected to our colleagues and ourselves. What better way to craft and deliver the right message to potential hires and new employees? The All Blacks show us that we can use rituals to grab others' attention before the games begin.

Onboarding Rituals with the Three P's in Mind: Psychological Safety + Purpose = Performance

Because the Three P's work together, it's crucial that we have to elicit a feeling of psychological safety and purpose from the very first touchpoints in the employee relationship. Doing so will positively impact future performance. From the very first contact with potential hires, we're setting the stage for success. Said another way, if we don't take advantage in the early days, we leave much on the table. But don't just take my word for it.

A 2018 survey by Kronos, a workforce solutions provider, found that "most companies view inductions as a way of informing new starters of rules and regulations. They pay lip service to the cultural aspects of the firm, but they don't give much time to when workers are most receptive."[10] Sounds like a wasted opportunity, right? London Business School professor Dan Cable set out to show just how big a waste it is with an experiment he and his colleagues conducted through a group of new call center hires at the tech company Wipro. Professor Cable and his colleagues created three groups of new employees:

1. One was given the company's standard induction, going over rules and regulations. (*Not very inspiring on any level.*)
2. The second was given a morale-boosting accomplishment-focused spiel about Wipro helping the new people feel proud to be part of the organization. (*Ok, but . . .*)
3. The third was asked to think about times in previous jobs when they themselves were proudest and then to discuss those memories with their group. Specifically, they were asked: "What is unique about you that leads you to your happiest times and best performance at work? Reflect on a

specific time—perhaps on a job or perhaps at home—when you were acting in the way that you were 'born to act.' " (*Now we're getting somewhere!*)

Six months later, employees from the third group were 32 percent more likely to remain in their jobs.[11] (Keep in mind here that replacing an employee costs anywhere from 50 to 200 percent of that employee's annual salary.[12]) The third group also had an 18 percent higher customer satisfaction rate.[13] In other words, the third group's performance rocked, especially in relation to the other groups.

Why would that be the case? The employees from the third group had the opportunity to reflect on their own best selves within the context of onboarding with Wipro, their new company. This ritual helped them genuinely *feel* like they belonged, as opposed to being told as much. They felt safe and secure. Trying to convince people they should feel proud to be part of a team doesn't work because it's just an idea. And it's not yet personal.

The Boston Consulting Group published a report in 2012 that ranked onboarding as having the second-highest impact out of all HR practices.[14] The first highest impact was "delivering on recruiting," or being adept at recruiting. The way to be adept at both recruiting and onboarding is to make them personal.

Some companies are so savvy with their rituals that they start rolling them out before—or as—the formal recruiting and onboarding process begins. You, too, can become one of the savvy ones.

So, let's start at the beginning of the beginning.

Preboarding with Rituals

You've probably heard of Zappos, the shoe company with the "fun and weird" culture that's landed it on *Fortune*'s 100 Best Companies to Work For many times. Even though Zappos leaders value fun, they take their recruiting very seriously. Recruiting is one of the most important ways they weave core values into the foundation of their business—their people.

One of my favorite rituals involves Zappos's approach to picking up potential hires at the airport. Someone from Zappos is assigned to fetch the out-of-towner in a Zappos-decorated van. The candidate is driven to the lobby for the interview, offered a drink of water and some snacks, and has some chit-chat to help put him at ease. Seems like pretty run-of-the-mill stuff, but here's the interesting part. The people at the front desk and the driver know that the recruiting team wants feedback, good or bad, about the potential hire, so they're all super-engaged, paying extra close attention to the personal behavior of the potential employee. One of Zappos's core values is "Be Humble," so they want to know if their interviewee is treating certain employees one way and their potential new boss or colleagues another.[15] This clever ritual helps to ensure that new hires are a good fit.

Sometimes a ride from the airport isn't just a ride from the airport!

At Zappos, recruiting rituals are a group endeavor. Other companies keep it simple with one-on-one, targeted wooing. Whatever approach companies take, every ritual is more effective when tied to company values.

Meet Kurt Varner, a designer who recounts his first contact with Dropbox, the online storage software company, as "a recruiting process that left me smiling." In the midst of his interview process, he visited the office repeatedly to do his own research on the company vibe. At one point, Varner was chatting with the design manager when he "noticed a bunch of folks from the design team walking out with champagne in hand, appearing to be in full party mode." He asked what they were celebrating, assuming it was a product release or something. "Nope," they said, "This is for you."[16]

It might not seem like such a big deal to offer a glass of bubbly to a new hire, but at that point Varner had not even accepted the Dropbox offer. You can rest assured, though—the toast certainly nudged him in that direction. He writes, "Dropbox was starting to feel like home," which, from a recruiting point of view, doesn't get any better.

But, wait, there's more; the Dropbox preboarding story doesn't end here.

When Varner got home that night, he found a little pink box on his apartment doorstep. "No shipping label, nothing. Just a small smiley face taped to the outside. I eagerly opened it to find a cupcake kit with a letter-pressed note from Dropbox expressing their excitement about the potential to have me join."

What's a cupcake kit, you ask?

At the time, Dropbox had five core values. The first four were: Be worthy of trust, Sweat the details, Aim higher, We not I, and the last one was just a picture of a cupcake, intended to signify the delight the company aspires to bring its customers.

So, naturally, the welcome package contained a letter-press invitation to join the company, as well as ingredients to make a cupcake.

Did Varner take the job? You bet he did.

This is a magical wooing ritual, not merely because I'm personally a sucker for tasty desserts and because it worked, but rather because of the way it is so cleverly tied into the company values.

Recruiting, interviewing, and hiring are all ripe opportunities for rituals. I admire and salute those companies that manage to think and move far ahead of the curve, as Dropbox did with the champagne and cupcake kit, because most companies don't really get their game on until official onboarding begins. But since recruiting begins with the very first contact a potential hire makes with your company, rituals can, too.

Day One Rituals

The first day of school is an iconic experience for all of us. We can all relate to the butterflies, great expectations, and stress about what to wear and where to sit. Will people like us? The first day of work is no different. And it only happens once. Smart companies use rituals to get it right.

Packages like the cupcake kit are popular welcoming rituals. The advertising giant Ogilvy offers a beautifully designed "induction box" to new hires. New employees at Adobe receive a "Kickbox" containing a Starbucks card and a $1,000 Mastercard.[17] Adobe's box also comes with a checklist of what to do in order to start pitching new ideas to the company. This onboarding ritual is so popular, Adobe has created an online guide (check out kickbox.org) for other companies who want to create a similar ritual for their own teams.

Branded boxes are a great way to bring new hires up to speed, but they can be pricey to produce. Simpler, low-cost welcomes work, too. Here are a couple of other options companies have adapted:

John Deere employees receive a simple email from a buddy on the current staff, giving first-day tips about what to wear and where to park.[18] I mean, who wants to show up in a suit when everyone else is wearing Hawaiian shirts?! Or to circle the employee parking lot worrying about being late? This first-day buddy later shows up at the newbie's desk with a welcome banner in tow. Radio Flyer is a Chicago-based family business that's been around for over a hundred years as makers of those iconic little red wagons (one of which sits in my own family's garage). Radio Flyer makes a very deliberate ritual out of giving new hires—what else?—their very own miniature "welcome" wagons, which would be a perfect gift in and of itself. But the thing that makes this ritual so special is the handwritten note that CEO (aka Chief "Wagon" Officer) Robert Pasin writes to each and every new hire, accompanied by a book on the family heritage of the company.

Glamsquad, an in-home hair and beauty service and my go-to for hair and makeup while on the road speaking, offers every new employee—including those in IT and finance—the opportunity to sit down in the NYC office salon and experience firsthand some kind of beauty treatment. I absolutely love thinking of the new guy from accounting getting his first pedicure on his first day on the job. He can't really refuse. It's a rite of passage. It's a Glamsquad ritual, connecting him to the culture.

IDEO, a global design firm, is determined to make new hires feel welcome. As part of the onboarding process, a new employee fills out a questionnaire about her favorite snacks before day one. Lo and behold, upon arrival, her desk is peppered with welcoming Post-its and her favorite go-to treats. In this way, IDEO makes work feel just like home, delivering a novel company-connecting take on comfort food.[19]

These simple gestures connect employees to the mission and purpose of the company, and in the case of Radio Flyer, also helps them feel seen by the CEO himself.

When it comes to rituals, a little goes a long way. Keep an eye out for what you already have at your disposal—wagons, beauty treatments, snacks—and see how you can ritualize your everyday.

Beyond the First Day

I'm all for tokens of appreciation, favorite snacks, and intentional coffee dates upon arrival. Day One and Week One celebrations are important for connecting, but it's important not to let the rituals go after people get up and running. The best beginnings go on and on, helping people find their way around their new life so that, hopefully, they'll stay awhile.

At KIND Snacks, founder and executive chairman Daniel Lubetzky has long determined to do one thing: create more kindness in the world. Lubetzky comes by his kindness honestly. His grandparents were saved from a Nazi invasion in Lithuania because Lubetzky's father had always been respectful to the apartment's superintendent charged with the evacuation. As Lubetzky puts it, "Because my grandfather had treated the superintendent with dignity, this person rose up. . . . It's a very weird feeling to know that I'm alive because of someone like that."[20]

Weird, wonderful, and impactful.

As a CEO, one of the ways he manifested this kindness is by maintaining a personal connection to his employees, even as his company grew to its current 700 team members.

KIND is a total Three P's place to work, as it's driven by a purpose, which is to "make the world a little kinder," and Lubetzky gets that the way to do this is to make sure people feel psychologically safe. Rituals work well on both counts.

Every quarter, Lubetzky gets together with the new hires, going around the table for *two or three hours* (that's a lot of time!), getting to know each other, getting to know him, and getting to know the history of KIND. Especially since they've grown so quickly year after year, they've had to create a curated space to get to know new hires and to help them bridge their past, present, and future. Elle Lanning, chief of staff and SVP of Corporate Development told me, "a really important part of who we were early on was that understanding of each person outside of what they were doing at KIND. . . . He sees me as Elle first, and a KIND team member second. That gets really hard as you scale, but we recognized the importance of it, so we moved to this quarterly approach, where all the new hires within that quarter came together." As a way of creating connection, Lubetzky asks employees to share something that most people wouldn't know about themselves, even if they had worked together for years, some kind of quirky detail or confession. Then—and I love this part— the group detects a pattern and names themselves. Maybe they're the "Clumsy Romantics" or the "Adventurers" or the "Funny Eaters."

But, wait, there's more! Each cohort gets a small budget to make a KIND-themed music video.

How fun is that? Plus, what better way to learn about the special talents of your colleagues, things you'd never learn otherwise? Lanning remembers the video she made years ago with the opera singer who happened to be in her cohort. As Lubetzky told me, "We're humanizing people."

Rituals sure can and do have that effect on people.

Patrick Vasquez is a general manager of Chipotle, the clean-fast-food giant whose growth is through the roof. In November 2019, their market value was $20.9 billion, up 74 percent since the year prior.[21] I visited his location on the Upper West Side in New York recently to learn about their rituals. He could not stop smiling—there are so many. He was introduced to his favorite on his own first day at Chipotle five years ago. "When we onboard new hires onto the team, they get a booklet, which is organized with all of their training materials so we can keep track and develop them over time. We call it the Yearbook." On their first day during orientation, new hires open up to the first page in their training guide and find that the local team has signed it with messages like, "Welcome to the team!" or "Welcome to Chipotle!"

As employees get promoted, their peers continue to write in the yearbook, and as Vasquez told me, the messages get more personal because they're more known. "Hearing from a General Manager, 'I remember hiring you, and I knew day one you would get to this point,' is just really special." He continued, "I still have my training guides, and I can look back at all of those pages and remember all of the faces I used to work with, all of the people that I've come by in the five years that I've been with this company."

This is exactly how a real ritual works—bringing people into the fold. It works so well because it's aligned with everything else Chipotle does. And everyone knows it. While Vasquez and I chatted, one of his crew members shared that the yearbook ritual is tied to the value "the movement is real," which gives his crew members a sense of purpose. And it can't hurt in providing psychological safety and belonging as well.

"My name is Cheryl. I'm a recruiter here at the Motley Fool, and people describe me as the 'Director of First Impressions.'" This is the beginning of my rituals conversation at Motley Fool, the quirky, hip, and cool financial firm.

Rituals are part of the fabric of Motley Fool. Cheryl told me, "New Fools are celebrated at Motley Fool in so many ways. As soon as they accept the job, they are asked to fill out a questionnaire with questions like: What's your favorite drink? What are your hobbies? What are your favorite movies? Favorite vacations? Do you have any pets? How do you want to commute to work?"

Then, after new Fools are given a big show of highly personalized love at their desk on the first day, a bowl of candy is placed there. Yes, it's celebratory, but as Kara Chambers, VP of People Insights, shared, it's highly intentional. "So someone comes up and says, 'I want a piece of candy, but I can't really get one until I talk to the new Fool. So I go and talk to the Fool and it's like, *Oh my God, you're new, and we have this in common!*' And all of a sudden, a tiny little Snickers has brought together two people."

The new person's desk is a ritualized snack bar.

To further enmesh the new Fools into the mix, Motley Fool has another ritual. The new Fools are tasked with walking around the office with a food cart for two hours sometime in their first month on the job so they can meet new people in different departments. Chambers put it like this: "People think, 'I never work on the tech team. I'm never really going to meet this person.' Suddenly you're at their desk with chips, and you are having a conversation."

Could there be more?! Yes, in addition, all new Fools are assigned a buddy—someone not on their team, but who has an explicit budget to take them out for lunch and coffee, which is pretty sweet. But the most impactful ritual is when the new Fools have coffee with the founders. Sometime during the first month of work, every single Fool sits down with brothers Tom and David Gardner, the dynamic founding duo. This opportunity is one of the rituals longtime Fools remember most. People ask each other, "Did you have your coffee yet with Tom and Dave?"

Cheryl recalls, "I remember it being so fun, and I remember being nervous, but they just make you feel so at ease, so at home." This is one ritual that everyone hears about and never misses.

Companies that have an intentional way of welcoming their new recruits start as they mean to go on. They understand that this is an opportunity to help new employees feel psychological safety, connected to purpose (their own and the company's), and ramp up to great performance. These are the Three P's in action!

So whether your onboarding efforts include a music video, a welcome wagon, or a snack cart, strive to be intentional in creating rituals that honor relationships from the very beginning.

✦ ✦ ✦ YIELD FOR RITUALS ✦ ✦

When onboarding, you only get one chance to make a first impression. That first day is critical, but it can't stop there. Get started by mapping out your recruiting and onboarding processes. Are there already rituals built in, and if so, are they working? Where are there opportunities for rituals? Which value(s) could you bake into the process—cupcakes are one approach to baking in values—but feel free to come up with your own company flavor.

Making every touchpoint count with rituals can help you decide who you want to hire, encourage potential employees to say yes, and then get them off and running on the right foot—feeling safe and connected.

RITUALS ROCKSTARS

Tom and David Gardner

For this chapter I chose to highlight Tom and David Gardner, brothers and founders of Motley Fool, as rituals rockstars. These two were camp counselors, which helps explain why they're *so good* at making rituals stick. In addition to all the fun they ritualize, they're ridiculously good storytellers. They and their team collect Fool stories, especially ones that emphasize their core values, then come together once a year to share them. Not only does this make for one heck of an engaging and culture-strengthening event, but it keeps Fools on the lookout for stories all year long. The big day harkens back to their camp days. They create a faux campfire in the office, invite someone to come in and sing with a guitar, and encourage Fools to gather 'round with sleeping bags and a tent.

Thanks, Gardner brothers, for being 100 percent you and bringing your love of rituals to work.

CHAPTER TWO

MARCH THROUGH THE ARCH

Rituals for Beginnings

Okay, job-seeker, you've got the job. Congratulations! And you, Manager—you've hired the next rockstar cohort. Well done!

After the balloons have deflated, the music video has been viewed, and the empty bowl of candy has been moved from the new person's desk, everyone defaults to just showing up at work.

Then what?

My goal in writing this book is to help transform "everyday routines" into "workplace magic," but that doesn't mean we'll *always* be having a blast. While that would be nice, it's not realistic. Sometimes work is actually, well, work. While we can and absolutely should feel plugged into a greater purpose beyond that looming checklist, we do need to make those calls (Yep! Good ol' fashioned phone calls), create that spreadsheet, and take our turn tidying up the communal kitchen. So where's the magic?

One of the ways rituals work best is by creating a container around the most mundane activities, thereby elevating them. Think about a wedding ceremony. There's nothing inherently commitment-worthy about a ring exchange or a single kiss. But because we grant those actions magical properties, they influence us to try to stay faithful and committed. Wedding traditions abound, from the beginning to the end, bookending the actual business of getting and staying married "till death do us part" (which the betrothed among us know is no piece of cake) with rituals.

This is how I think about rituals at work, too. There's the requisite business of being in business, and then there are the rituals that help us power up and through the day—the work of work. So for this next stop on our roadmap, we're shining a light on beginnings and endings.

Leadership and management writer Gwen Moran writes in a *Fast Company* article, "Rituals signal to us that it's time for a specific mindset or activity. They act as triggers to more effortlessly get us ready for what we need to do."[1] Rituals are great preparation, and they can help us wrap things up, too. After all, the end of one thing is the beginning of another. These days, with our jobs chasing after us, pinging from our pockets at all hours of every day if we let them, taking time off is a mindset that needs our attention more than ever. Put another way: If we don't take charge of our schedules, our devices will happily do it for us. We can harness rituals at the beginning and end of everything we do, and we can ensure we include our technology, leveraging what we love about it, while also putting it in its place.

As you read through these rather clever ideas, think about how you begin—perhaps a day, a week, a meeting, or a project—and for whom. Perhaps just yourself, your team, or your company. I'll share great beginning rituals here, and some of my favorite closing rituals at the end of the book. Whether we do the same thing at the beginning and the end of an activity, akin to the "Om" chanted at the beginning and end of a yoga class, or something different, like how we begin standing at attention at a baseball game with the "Star-Spangled Banner" and end with the seventh-inning stretch, one thing is for sure: beginnings and endings are prime ritual real estate.

Opening Ceremonies

Perhaps the most illustrious of all opening ceremonies is the incredible pomp and circumstance of the Olympics, some of which dates all the way back to the ancient Greek games. Today, the official commencement of the most comprehensive international gathering on earth takes place with the parade of nations. Athletes from around the world march in alphabetical order according to the host's language, including the number of strokes in Chinese translations. This is just one of many ways the Olympics make an effort to include the value of diversity into the rituals.

And then, of course, there's the torch-runner, perhaps one of the most well-known rituals on earth.

As we know, the summer Olympics of 2020 were postponed due to COVID-19. So what's an Olympics fan to do? One of my favorite rituals while we were quarantined was to watch the women's Olympic gymnastics team and individual all-around finals with my daughters starting with the 1996 Olympics in Atlanta. We do what we can, right? And rituals help us ease the pain.

For most of us who report to an office, our opening ceremonies kind of naturally evolve—we walk out of the elevator into the office, grabbing a coffee along the way. For those who work from home, it's helpful to think about how to create personal opening ceremonies to help start the day and delineate home from work.

Not an easy task! But rituals can really help us create the transitions that have never mattered more.

For years companies have been abandoning traditional offices, sometimes for coworking spaces, and other times for at least partly remote arrangements. In 2018, "flexible workspaces accounted for more than two-thirds of the U.S. office market occupancy gains," and "by 2030, the flexible workspace market is expected to represent 30 percent of U.S. office stock."[2] According to an OWL Lab survey on remote workers, 62 percent work remotely (30 percent being completely full time), compared to the 38 percent of employees that work solely on-site.[3]

Wow!

Does this mean that unless you have to punch a time clock or show up in an office, work never really begins and never really ends? No, not at all. In fact, I would argue that because so many more of us are expected to be our own DIY supervisor, appreciation for beginnings and endings matters, a lot. Regardless of where you sit or what time it is, rituals are the perfect way to light the torch on your own Olympics, signaling to yourself and others that work has begun.

Monday, a Beautiful Thing?

Whether you work at work, at home, or what many called the Third Space, Starbucks or another public space, Monday is Monday, and for many people, it's the official beginning of the workweek. One of my personal rituals for years has been to take an hour on Sunday night to organize my thoughts, identify work and family priorities, and even check a few things off my list so I can hit the ground running on Monday.

Sara Blakely is famous for a couple things. She came up with the idea for Spanx, the shapewear sensation. And in 2012 she became the world's youngest self-made female billionaire.[4] I'm willing to bet that her personal rituals play a role in her success.

One awesome Sara Blakely ritual is that Mondays are her "think day." She keeps them unstructured, with no meetings so she can begin the week with some space. But don't let that lead you to believe that the rest of her week is back-to-back without any time or space to think. Blakely actually begins every day with one of my favorite rituals—ever! As she told Reid Hoffman on his awesome podcast, *Masters of Scale*, "I live really close to Spanx, so I've created what my friends call my 'fake commute,' and I get up an hour early before I'm supposed to go to Spanx, and I drive around aimlessly in Atlanta with my commute so that I can have my thoughts come to me."[5]

Don't you love thinking of this powerhouse CEO driving around the Atlanta suburbs just thinking?

While spending all these hours by herself, dreaming up the next big thing, may seem like a waste of time, the numbers speak for themselves—Spanx has grown to an estimated $400 million in sales.[6]

Indulgence never looked so productive.

Another CEO that has taken to Monday indulgences is Jodi Kovitz, the founder and CEO of #movethedial, a company devoted to changing the story of women in tech. Today Kovitz has 22 employees, and she begins each Monday with a ritual that she started when she had only two.

At 9:30 a.m. on Monday mornings, her team comes together for what Kovitz calls a "grounding ritual," in order to "connect on a human level, and to invest in the culture and connectivity of the team."

Each person shares three things: (1) something they're grateful for, personal or professional, (2) something they're proud of, and (3) something that they're struggling with.

The ritual began as just part of the meeting, which would then transition to business updates, but people were so into the Monday morning ritual that Kovitz moved the status updates to their own meeting on Thursday.

Wouldn't it make more business sense to launch the week with projects and bottom-line projections? Well, in case you haven't heard, the soft stuff is the new hard stuff. And for Kovitz, "It's more important for people to feel glued together, connected, grounded, valued—like they have a reason to be there. And to ease into Monday is really a beautiful thing."[7]

Google's Project Aristotle was an extensive study of 180+ teams over two years to find out what makes teams great. They found that teams that feel psychologically safe (the first and most important of five attributes that make up a great team) are rated effective twice as much by their leaders. Not only that, but these teams bring in more revenue, demonstrate more innovation, and have better retention.[8] And as Promise54, a nonprofit talent solutions provider, reminds us, "Psychological safety is critical to DEI work [diversity, equity, and inclusion] because it supports and enables vulnerability, learning, growth, and behavior change."[9]

Psychological safety really moves the dial on performance.

Monk Mode Mornings

Rituals are a great way to begin the week with intention. The same, though, goes for the beginning of any given day. Georgetown computer science professor and technology and culture expert, Cal Newport, in his book *Deep Work*, writes, "I'm starting to see more entrepreneurs . . . especially CEOs of small startups—doing what I call Monk Mode Morning, where they say, 'As far as anyone is concerned I'm reachable starting at 11 a.m. or noon, and I am never available for meetings, I'm never going to answer an email and never going to answer the phone before then."[10] Holding off on connecting with others helps us connect to ourselves first.

In his blog post about the topic, Newport underscores the reason Monk Mode Mornings work so well: "What makes this hack particularly effective is its simple regularity. If someone wants to schedule something with you, it becomes reflexive to respond 'anytime after noon.' Similarly, your colleagues soon learn not to expect you to see something they send until after lunch."[11] Did you catch that? The magic is in the ritual of it. Monk Mode Morning is a personal working ritual that first honors your relationship with yourself by prioritizing your deep, focused work. Then by proxy it's a ritual that helps your colleagues honor their working relationship with you by respecting your intentional boundaries. Win-win.

Top leaders are known for being disciplined, often including some variation of Monk Mode Morning behavior. Ron Ben-Zeev, founder and CEO of World Housing Solution, a provider of structures for the armed forces, prefers to be the first one to arrive at his office. "Coming in before anyone else is in the office makes me more productive. I've found that for me, working one hour alone is equal to two hours in the office with people because there are no distractions and no one pulling you."[12] Anyone with kids knows how important it is to be the first one up in order to get anything accomplished. There's nothing better than a quiet morning, an early-riser ritual, to collect one's thoughts.

Take a guess how Rich Pierson, cofounder of the meditation app Headspace, starts his day. Sure enough, he always start his day with 60 minutes of meditation. "I have done this consistently for almost nine years now, and it's the foundation for everything I do," he admits.[13] Since its founding in 2010, Headspace has been downloaded 62 million times in 190 countries and boasts more than 2 million paid subscribers.[14] Whether it's the ritual or just the meditating, it sure looks like something's working!

If meditating isn't your jam, you could try what Lara Little, founder and CEO of Lusomé, a luxury sleepwear company, does. "I carve out 30 minutes every morning to sit quietly with a cup of hot lemon water and set my intention for the day. No iPhone or email either—just my thoughts, a pen and my favorite Muji journal. I've also stopped trying to cram in 25 daily tasks and instead focus on three meaningful goals that can be related to business, family, health, or social good. It's so gratifying to cross them off my list and gives me a small sense of accomplishment every single day."[15]

Or you can do what Sara Blakely does and factor some "me time" into your commute. As Blakely told Hoffman, "I've identified where my best thinking happens, and it's in the car," and I think that is true for many of us—that solo, unstructured time like when we're in the shower. Sometimes we just need to make sure that these spaces stay private. Ritualizing these in-between spaces keeps them sacred.

The key with these individual rituals is to find what works for you. Find out when your brain is at its peak creativity, and carve out that time to sit with yourself and focus on your work. The term *meditation* often is associated with sitting quietly, legs crossed, with your mind completely shut off. But that's not what meditation is. Meditation as an individual ritual is about connecting to yourself and understanding what you need to do your best work. This can be as simple as spending a few hours of the day focusing on your own work, collecting your thoughts in a journal, or listening to music on your daily commute.

Virtual Beginnings

It's hard to imagine the Olympics opening over Zoom, but remote companies have been doing it like this forever, and they have a lot to teach us.

Dribbble is an online community for designers to connect with each other and for those seeking design services. I had a blast chatting with CEO Zack Onisko, especially about rituals that help his entire remote workforce feel connected.

Onisko explained, "We don't really have very strict working hours. We try to leverage their remote work lifestyle to allow people to be able to build their perfect day and kind of come online and leave as they need to." This could lead to a pretty chaotic beginning of the workday, particularly given different time zones. Instead, a simple, oddly organic ritual has grown at Dribbble to keep employees feeling linked to one another.

At the beginning and end of the workday, people simply log onto the company Slack channel and say hi, waving to their colleagues with an emoji. Some people even invite their remote colleagues into a more intimate Zoom room to drink coffee together.

In addition, on Fridays, the morning ritual gets powered up. Instead of just a little wave, people share a photo of themselves in the moment or from the past, sometimes in work attire and, well, sometimes wearing a prom dress! Do you remember the one question that I always asked during my research to identify great company rituals? When I asked Nicole Warshauer, director of branding communications, this question—*What is it at Dribbble that makes you feel most like a Dribbble-employee or most "Dribbble-ish"?*—she didn't miss a beat, "Friday mornings are the most Dribbble-ish for me."

With connecting wave-and-photo-rituals like these, it's not hard to see why *Inc.* magazine identified Dribbble as "one of the 5,000 fastest-growing private companies in America in 2020."[16]

Whether your opening ceremony has always been stopping at Starbucks every morning (like me), meditating, sharing with your team, or turning on your computer and waving, beginnings matter, so think about how you can work with your employees to make them meaningful. Opening ceremony rituals aren't just important for your employees to feel connected, they can also impact your customers by inviting them into your world.

A Customer Walks into a Store

Rituals is a Dutch-based home and cosmetics company that operates in 31 countries and counting. As of May 2019, there were 730 stores around the world, and Rituals was opening 2.5 stores a week (120 a year) when most retailers have been closing stores left and right. Marjolein Westerbeek, the president of Rituals USA, shared with me that they, in fact, "don't consider themselves a retailer." Rather, their very purpose is to be in the business of creating rituals—hence, the name. They're on a mission to transform everyday routines into rituals magic.

When you walk into a Rituals store anywhere in the world, you're first offered a cup of tea. Receiving tea and not a sales pitch is something the company does intentionally, and something that certainly made me feel connected when I walked into the store. Secondly, each customer is offered a "meaningful moment." It could be a one-minute meditation. It could be a hand massage. There are a number of different ways that the employees strive to create opportunities to pause. It's only after those two things have happened that employees even start thinking and talking about the products. They view the products as a catalyst to create more meaningful moments, aka, *purpose.*

Westerbeek reflected on why she's so patient, so willing to press pause before the pitch. "The mission has always been the same, but bringing meaningful moments and rituals to people and telling their stories takes time."

These rituals are worth the wait.

Laura Mignott is the founder and CEO of DFlash, an event-planning company in New York City. Mignott, like Westerbeek, understands from personal experience how important it is to bring people in thoughtfully and to promote feelings of safety and belonging from the very beginning. She told me, "This might happen more to me being a black woman in business, where a lot of times I don't feel welcome. It could be I'm being followed around Barney's, or people will just be ignoring me at a store. It's ridiculous . . . and often at events. It happens all the time, still."

How does she combat this potential unwelcome feeling, professionally and for people attending her events? And how does she create the opposite experience, one where people feel like they belong? Some of the simplest rituals are the most powerful. She makes it her business (literally) to stand at the front door of the events and say, "Welcome home." Sometimes people ask her if she lives there, at the event space, to which she responds, " 'Yes! It's my house!' It's an amuse-bouche, like a palate cleanser. People smile."

Still not sure that something so simple and homespun can actually make a difference? In support, Mignott responded,

"The proof is in the pudding. When we worked with Samsung for about five to six years, we transformed their experience at SXSW . . . to where they were the coolest thing at South-by. Not by investing a ton of money, but by changing how people perceive the ritual of going into the experience for Samsung."

The DFlash website summarizes, "Our motto is simple: Welcome Home—every experience we create should feel welcoming when you walk thru the door & should feel like home, so that you'll want to stay."[17]

For Mignott, helping people feel safe and welcome is her purpose. Sometimes it's something as simple as a hello that stops someone in their tracks. Their motto is simple, and it works.

March Through the Arch—and Then Do It Again: Bookending Rituals

If a ritual works well once, why not do it again? I like the concept of bookending rituals around important events. Applying a ceremony to an ending can be incredibly powerful. The Olympics, for example, always ends with just as much pomp and circumstance as in the beginning. The parade of flags, the host country's national anthem—many of the opening rituals return to close the circle.

When Morty Schapiro made the move from the president of Williams College to Northwestern University in the summer of 2009, one of his very first meetings was with the office of Student Affairs. Schapiro asked, "What are our long-standing traditions?" The response he heard underwhelmed: "What traditions?"

While Northwestern is a newer school, less steeped in age-old traditions than Williams College and other East Coast institutions, Schapiro felt it was important to identify and amplify existing Northwestern rituals and create new ones.

Schapiro soon uncovered a few. Painting the Rock is one where students from various campus groups have been painting a rock with lines like "Pledge Kappa" or "Come to Club

Lacrosse" since 1957. Dillo Day, an all-day rock festival on the water every May on the Saturday before exams is another. But Schapiro soon realized that Northwestern didn't have a ritual to welcome incoming students. We all know how important onboarding is, so he went back to Student Affairs and asked for help. A colleague suggested, "Let's walk the kids through the arch that's on campus." A ritual was born.

Schapiro and his team rushed to quickly organize a march through the arch in September 2009. They didn't bother getting permission from the city that first year, which turned out not to be a problem, since only about 20 kids participated, and they just dodged the cars to march through the arch.

By year three, every single incoming student—over 2,000 kids—marched through the arch. Today, it's a ritual not to be missed. The marching band leads the students through Weber Arch, so named by Schapiro for his predecessor and the fourteenth president of the university, Arnie Weber.[18]

Rituals do well when steeped in tradition.

These days parents, told in advance where to find their kids in the sea of purple, line the streets and take pictures. The kids feel like they are part of something special as they walk through the arch like all those who came before them and begin to come together as their own class. When I visited Northwestern, students told me that the march makes them feel more connected to their classmates and the university. I'm sure the same goes for the parents who are kvelling from the sidelines.

Recently, Northwestern added the back end of this ritual, welcoming its graduating students back through the arch during graduation week for a full-circle journey. In 2018 only about a third of the class (or 700 kids) actually walked back through the arch, but it's a work in progress moving in the right direction—bookending one of life's most important times.

And here's the kicker: Even though the march through the arch is a relatively recent ritual, the students don't see it this way. Schapiro once asked a student, "What is your proudest moment so far at Northwestern?" The student's response: "My best moment that brought me to tears was March through the

Arch because to be part of such a grand old tradition really touched my soul."

As Schapiro told me with a twinkle in his eye, "I didn't have the heart to tell him that it was only the third year."

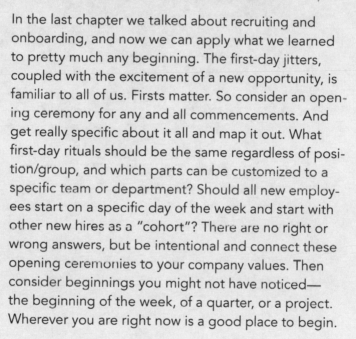

YIELD FOR RITUALS

In the last chapter we talked about recruiting and onboarding, and now we can apply what we learned to pretty much any beginning. The first-day jitters, coupled with the excitement of a new opportunity, is familiar to all of us. Firsts matter. So consider an opening ceremony for any and all commencements. And get really specific about it all and map it out. What first-day rituals should be the same regardless of position/group, and which parts can be customized to a specific team or department? Should all new employees start on a specific day of the week and start with other new hires as a "cohort"? There are no right or wrong answers, but be intentional and connect these opening ceremonies to your company values. Then consider beginnings you might not have noticed— the beginning of the week, of a quarter, or a project. Wherever you are right now is a good place to begin.

RITUALS ROCKSTAR

Radha Agrawal

Radha Agrawal is the author of the amazing book *Belong: Find Your People, Create Community and Live a More Connected Life*, an international speaker, and founder of Daybreaker, the early-morning dance party enjoyed by 500,000 people in 30 cities around the world.

Her book opens with a bang: "When I turned thirty, I realized I didn't belong." And that was from someone with an identical twin![19]

This revelation happened in a sports bar where she saw that "people were looking around the room and not at one another. Half the bar was buried in their phones, and the other half was belligerently drunk . . ."[20]

It was this wake-up call that inspired her to devote her life to becoming a "Community Architect," and to launch Daybreaker, a nonalcoholic ritual-fest. Not only is the morning party a ritual for many, but the event itself is filled with rituals, especially around beginnings and endings.

Last October I went to a Daybreaker party in order to see what all the fuss was about—how Agrawal manages to lure tens of thousands of people to line up for a DJ'd boogie before work.

Now, these parties happen all over the world at different times, so imagine my surprise when Agrawal herself was there! I recognized her and immediately went over to her, introduced myself, and told her all about my book.

And then she shouted over the music, with her baby—wearing headphones that protect hearing at a loud event—strapped around her body, "Rituals are everything!"

Yes!

I couldn't have said it better myself. The Daybreaker tagline is "start your day with energy & intention,"[21] and that's what rituals do for us—set us on the path of energetic intention.

When she launched Daybreaker, Agrawal wanted to design "distinct" rituals when its participants (which she calls community members) enter and exit a Daybreaker event. "Instead of mean bouncers looking you up and down, we have a 'Hugging Committee.' Every single person gets a hug and a 'Good morning!' when they walk in. This creates instant camaraderie, and releases

(continued)

oxytocin . . . activated through human touch."[22] Agrawal says that she has probably hugged over 10,000 community members at this point and that she knows how important this ritual is based on "the number of people who have thanked [her] afterward and shared they were nervous about going alone or were going through stuff and needed a hug."[23]

Like me, many were nervous coming alone.

Upon exiting a Daybreaker event, each person receives an intention card which is read aloud as a group. At the Daybreaker event I attended, the front of the card said: *How Will You Set Your Fall Intentions?* Then as a group, Agrawal asked us to flip the card over and read aloud the following quote by Yoko Ono:

> *Spring passes and one remembers one's innocence.*
> *Summer passes and one remembers one's exuberance.*
> *Autumn passes and one remembers one's reverence.*
> *Winter passes and one remembers one's perseverance.*

Walking away from Agrawal and Daybreaker, I couldn't stop thinking about all the sweaty people grinning ear to ear on their way . . . to work! I could only imagine what kind of inspiration they would carry into their next beginning.

Was I surprised when I got the email a couple of months later announcing that Daybreaker was going on tour with Lady Gaga, Jennifer Lopez, Oprah, and Michelle Obama as the morning ritual-exertainment?

Not even a little.

Why not? Because CEO and cofounder Radha Agrawal is not just a rituals rockstar, she's a *total rockstar*.

CHAPTER THREE

MEETINGS

Rituals for Gatherings That Matter

'm willing to wager that you attended *at least* one work-related meeting in the last 48 hours. Were you engaged the whole time? Did you notice your colleagues scrolling through their phones, answering emails, browsing Facebook, doing anything *but* contributing to and focusing on the discussion? Were you doing any of those things? Cut to March of 2020, when—overnight—employees everywhere were in Zoom meetings all day, adding yet another challenge to meeting well.

Rituals can help make all of our gatherings matter whether they're in person, remote, or somewhere in between.

Before the COVID crisis hit, experts like Harvard Business School professor Nancy Koehn estimated that approximately 11 million formal meetings were held in US workplaces each day.[1] Average employees sat through roughly 62 meetings every month.[2] The more you're promoted, the more meetings you can expect to attend. (Oh, the things to look forward to!) I'm sure I don't have to tell you that people frequently check out of these meetings. And when we're sitting through that many meetings a month, who could blame them? What's more, Doodle, the online meeting service, reported that meetings cost the United States over \$399 billion in lost productivity in 2019.[3] Having a hard time imagining how much money that is? According to *Wired* magazine, that's about the same cost required to build 47,000 miles of the interstate highway system.[4]

Are we really prepared to spend that kind of time and potentially wasted money on a bunch of meetings where people scroll surreptitiously through their Instagram feeds under the table? Leaders, please take this very seriously. A person's time is a terrible (and very expensive) thing to waste.

To be more precise, what are some of the consequences of having employees suffer through poorly organized meetings? According to the Doodle report mentioned above, respondents from around the world complained:

- Poorly organized meetings mean I don't have enough time to do the rest of my work (44 percent).
- Unclear actions lead to confusion (43 percent).

- Bad organization results in a loss of focus on projects (38 percent).
- Irrelevant attendees slow progress (31 percent).
- Inefficient processes weaken client/supplier relationships (26 percent).

Personally, one of the biggest gripes I hear from people is that they can't get their "real work" done until their meetings are over at 5 or 6 p.m. Are we destined to move mindlessly through our day, trudging crankily from meeting to meeting?

No way, says Priya Parker, founder of Thrive Labs and author of *New York Times* bestseller *The Art of Gathering: How We Meet and Why It Matters* (one of my all-time favorite books). She writes, "Gathering—the conscious bringing together of people for a reason—shapes the way we think, feel, and make sense of our world . . . we spend our lives gathering."[5] We can't help ourselves! I've always been touched by the fact that we humans still love to meet, even when it's making us crazy and/or unproductive. That's why it's so important that we bring rituals to our meetings, making the most of the human urge to sit together, face-to-face (including via Skype, Facetime, and Zoom), and collaborate. We can do this in two ways: first by having a purpose, and second by inviting presence. Just think of your own meetings. When people are there for a reason and are both physically and psychologically present, meetings are, well, better. And as is always true, rituals that are linked to values are even more effective.

You might assume, as many do, that some groups would rather skip face-to-face meetings altogether. We often hear that millennials and Gen Zers would prefer to ditch in-person meetings in favor of Slack, text, or email. OK, but not so fast, Boomer! My friend and multigenerational workplace expert Lindsey Pollak reminds us, "The stereotype about millennials and Gen Zers is that they prefer to communicate through technology, which sometimes they do (and don't we all these days?). But they don't want to communicate through technology *all* of the time, and that is a big mistake that I see managers, even the best intentioned, making. . . . They have everyone dial into conference calls from their individual desks instead of all sitting in a conference room together to participate." From Boomers to Gen Zers, we all want and need to gather. The digital pull is strong, but we must continue to allow for, even to prioritize, in-person connection whenever we can, and rituals can lead us in that direction.

There's real science to back this up. When we sit together and solve a problem, when we get a new idea, or laugh, or move the needle on some big thinking we're doing, our feel-goods go up, and our stress goes down. When safety and purpose are present on a team, our brains release oxytocin—the feel-good hormone.[6] Once the oxytocin is released in our brains, "the enhanced empathy enabled by oxytocin allows humans to quickly form teams and work together effectively."[7] How's that for (hormonally harnessing) magic? According to social neuroscientist Pascal Vrticka, this dates all the way back to "evolutionary processes [that] have favored the development of complex social behaviors in humans, along with the brain architecture that supports them."[8] We are quite literally wired to connect.

If you're reading along, remembering the last meeting you endured, thinking . . . *sure, right, it's magic* . . . hang in there. In this chapter I'll help you see how. And looking back to Chapter Two where I shared Northwestern's marching through the arch tradition, be sure to remember: every meeting is better when you open and close strong.

More Than Assembly Is Required: Have a Purpose

The word *meeting* is defined as "an assembly of people, especially the members of a society or committee for discussion or entertainment."

But here's the thing: "assembling" is for Ikea furniture. Mere assembling is not going to make magic happen. With rituals we can transform everyday assemblies into workplace magic.

Now, before you respond with something I hear a lot—
But don't some meetings just have to be boring?—here's what
Parker has written: "The more habitual the meeting, the more
important it is to pause and ask, why are we gathering in the first
place?" It might seem obvious why you're meeting, but Parker
urges us to push beyond knee-jerk responses such as, "We're
meeting to share information and get an update." In *The Art
of Gathering*, Parker writes about "the great paradox of gathering: There are so many good reasons for coming together that
often we don't know precisely why we are doing so."[9] She urges
us to begin every meeting by knowing its purpose: Why are
we meeting? She calls this the "Passover Principle" evoking the
ritual question asked on that holy holiday—*Why is this night
different from all other nights?*[10] In determining our purpose,
Parker asserts, "specificity is a crucial ingredient."

Creating a super-specific purpose may seem counterintui-
tive or dangerously exclusive. Don't we want our meetings to
cover a lot of ground and be open to all? Quite the opposite,
according to Parker. "The more focused and particular a gathering is, the more narrowly it frames itself and the more passion
it arouses."[11] Parker has seen that this is true in her own work,
and I have, too. "Status updates" are important, but we ought
not to have a meeting to discuss something that can be sent
out in an email or viewed on a company dashboard. Meetings
with a specific purpose have another benefit. They will (hopefully) limit attendance to those who have something to add to
that very specific topic. Scott Heiferman, the former CEO of
Meetup, an online platform that has helped millions of people
gather, agrees. "LGBTQIA+ couples hiking with dogs" will be
a more successful meet-up than "LGBTQIA+ couples hiking,"
or "couples hiking with dogs," or even "LGBTQIA+ hikers
with dogs." Parker believes a meeting's purpose should "stick
its neck out a little."[12] The way I see it, having a very clear mission for each meeting creates a stronger feeling of belonging
than a "come one, come all" invitation.

Rituals can help us elevate our meetings to become something nobody wants to miss.

Survival Through Mutual Support

In my last book, *Bring Your Human to Work*, I highlighted A+I, the award-winning design firm responsible for many spectacular work environments, including Squarespace's and Horizon Media's stunning headquarters in Manhattan. A+I's founders, Brad Zizmor and Dag Folger (both ritual fanatics), each amazing in their own right, have become award winners as a pair. They've survived two recessions, and the intervening ups and downs of being in business together for 24 years is not unlike a successful marriage. What's their secret? If I knew I'd bottle it. But one remarkable ritual has certainly kept them bonded through the years: They have a breakfast meeting together every Monday, only to be missed under "extenuating circumstances." It's always at 8:30 a.m. and always at the same place, a restaurant near their office. This meeting moves way beyond practical assembly. It's an exercise in devotion; it's a ritual.

COVID-19 led to such extreme extenuating circumstances that all restaurants in NYC were closed, and Zizmor and Folger could no longer meet—anywhere!—for their 8:30 a.m. breakfast. I reached out to Zizmor in the middle of the pandemic to check in, ask how the business was holding up and how they individually and collectively were doing. This is what he said: "Breakfast with Dag is one of the things I miss the very most about not going into the office. It's amazing how environments and spaces affect how we think and feel."

I asked if he and Dag still have their weekly ritual. "We continue our tradition on a long weekly phone call. It's interesting for us that it's on the phone, not video conference, where we connect more deeply like we did before at the Monday breakfast. One day soon we shall resume the ritual in the restaurant as before with the hubbub, which it turns out didn't distract us. Rather it kept us focused!"

So, what exactly is the purpose of Zizmor and Folger's highly ritualized meeting—whether in person or on the phone? As Zizmor put it, even though the details change from week to week, the agenda is always the same: "Survival through mutual support." Survival through mutual support has never mattered more.

As Zizmor told me during our original interview, "We want the next 24 years to be as entrepreneurial as our first. And you have to earn that, right? . . . I think it's something that you have to put your mind to. It's like exercise . . . you have to really commit."

Zizmor and Folger's Monday morning ritual is a "recommitment to each other." Are some meetings spent looking at bottom-line metrics? Sure, but as Zizmor knowingly told me, "The metrics are our support, and that trickles down. I see it in new hires and how they treat each other." And it's in these new hires' behavior that the Third P of Performance really shines.

To have two guys' breakfast ritual trickling throughout an 80-person firm is pretty magical.

Don't Say We Didn't Warn You

Basecamp is an amazing web-based project-management tool with a whopping 3.3 million accounts set up since 2004 and "tens of millions of dollars in annual profits."[13] I used Basecamp for myself and my small team when my business was growing. The headquarters of the company's 50-person workforce is in Chicago, but most of the team works remotely. The CEO, Jason Fried, is the author of several books, including one of my favorites, *It Doesn't Have to Be Crazy at Work*, and *Remote*. I guess you could say that Fried literally wrote the book on remote work. Using a variety of ritualized meetings is one of his most important tricks of the trade.

Twice a year, everyone from Basecamp gathers in Chicago for a weeklong meet-up. The purpose of this important meeting is the single most important thing any company can do, and that's to "meet up" intentionally. Between shared breakfasts and lunches, Basecampers attend sessions and workshops, play Ping-Pong, and get to know each other. Only one companywide dinner is scheduled, and that occurs on Tuesdays. Wednesdays, by the way, include pizza and Dungeons and Dragons, for those interested. You get the picture.

Yes, work gets done. But the main purpose is to be together, which is terrific for some but can feel overwhelming for others. The employee handbook section called "Our Rituals" contains advice for meet-up burnout: "We're interacting all day with coworkers when we're used to working from home. We're having fun and perhaps not getting much sleep. Remember that the meet-up is what you want it to be. If you want to skip dinner one night, skip dinner and take a bath in your hotel room. If you need some recharge time, and want to work from a coffee shop one afternoon, do it! If you want to go to the tiki bar at 2 a.m., don't say we didn't warn you."[14]

Connecting is not a one-size-fits-all purpose.

Flying people in from all across the globe and putting them in hotels twice a year for them to connect is a significant investment for a small company. And it speaks volumes to the importance of this meeting ritual.

Another important purpose-driven Basecamp ritual is the once-a-year mini-meet-up that people can choose to participate in "at the destination of your choosing." This meeting walks a pretty nuanced line: "They're not meant to be social trips, and you're not doing just your day-to-day work in the same room as your coworkers. You should be collaborating on something meaningful. It certainly doesn't have to be big and you don't have to produce something by the end of the meet-up. Pick something you'd love to have a week to discuss in person and have fun with it."[15]

Finally, Basecamp celebrates with a ritual called the 5x12s. Every month, five employees are selected to chat on a call with Fried and his partner, cofounder and CTO David Heinemeier Hansson. The purpose for the 5x12s? "These calls are supposed to be fun, so please try to have a good time with them! . . . Some interesting topics that have been covered in the past: Jamie's $1,000 toilet, Wailin's Ted Cruz sighting, and petty juvenile delinquency stories from an alarming number of employees."[16] Because this ritual is such a chill call, participants don't have to do anything to prepare except for one thing: "Putting on pants—please put on pants."

Your Physical, Mental, and Spiritual Presence Is Requested

Now that you know that your meeting has to have a purpose, you have to be sure people actually show up, not just in body, but in mind, and even spirit. Presence is a prerequisite for psychological safety and helps ensure that your purpose manifests. It doesn't matter how well you've planned your meeting if everyone is scrolling mindlessly and spacing out. Yes, even if they have their pants on.

The best meetings invite people to bring their presence into the room, and there are rituals to help us do that. I like the idea of chiming in and chiming out of meetings as a way of waking people up and bringing them to the present.

Francesca Gino, one of the authors of the "Don't Stop Believin'" study from the Introduction, reports nearly half of 400 people surveyed online said they perform rituals before doing an anxiety-provoking task, which some meetings are for many of us. One participant wrote that before going to work or stepping into a meeting, he tries "to remove any negative energies" by pounding his feet on the ground several times and shaking his body.[17]

That's one approach!

And here's another:

One of the most watched TED talks in history is Amy Cuddy's talk on how "power posing" changes perception.[18] By putting our hands on our hips like Wonder Woman, a quintessential "high power" pose, we can "summon an extra surge of power and sense of well-being when it's needed," which is another way of saying that "fake it till you make it" is scientifically backed, great advice![19]

A very introverted, socially anxious friend of mine always goes into the bathroom to power pose before meetings. That's her ritual. Nobody would ever guess she's nervous. I guess her ritual works.

Chiming In

Before jumping into the news and status of the day part of your meeting, it's always a good idea to take a moment to gather people together, asking them to leave whatever they were doing before at the door. A chime is like an "Enter Here" signal.

Eileen Fisher, the fashion queen of comfy-chic, rings a literal chime at the beginning of meetings. The chime signals a minute of silence and meditation prior to a meeting commencing. She finds that "across the company—designers and merchandisers and advertising people, and people in the supply chain—the passion around this work has gotten a lot deeper." How can a moment of mindfulness go this far and this deep? Fisher asserts, "Because I think when people start to pay attention to themselves, they start to pay attention to their relationships, to the people around them and how they treat each other, and they start to notice the people in the supply chain."[20] I get it. As soon as we feel safe enough to become more aware of ourselves, we begin to see our impact.

In this simple example it certainly looks as though with one tiny ritual, people begin to feel psychologically safe and connected to purpose, which helps their performance. Fisher has even found that these Three P's have created a community empowered to change what Fisher herself has called the "nasty fashion industry." That's good news for all of us.

Fisher isn't the only one. Remember diversity and inclusion expert Daisy Auger-Dominguez from the Introduction? She's found that chiming in with norms that solidify trust and safety from the very beginning of meetings are essential for them to be productive, culture-reflecting, and nurturing. She chatted with me about her time at Viacom as the SVP of Talent Acquisition where she opted to, "rotate 'leader' for meetings amongst [her] leadership team and encouraged them to do the same with their own reports." I asked her how that might work, and she continued, "For example, the week that it was my head of operations' turn to lead our team meeting, she could designate someone from her team. That person was responsible for selecting themes to discuss in addition to our standard updates, speakers, etc. [It was a] great way to share situational privilege in meetings and also a great learning opportunity about the challenges of ensuring voice, managing different speaking and learning styles, business priorities, etc."[21] This kind of approach doesn't just *invite* everyone to chime in, it demands it. And that's what real D&I needs—no excuses. Chiming in, in this case, with D&I in mind, is a particularly good step in the right direction.

Another wonderful chiming-in-like ritual comes from one of my favorite corporate rituals all-stars, LinkedIn, which you'll read more about in Chapter Five on professional development. Because culture is such an important part of LinkedIn's success, they have no problem attracting volunteers to serve as "culture champions," a group of people in charge of the over-the-top-inspiring life at LinkedIn. To be chosen as a champion is both an honor and a privilege, so much so that Nawal Fakhoury, senior manager of employee experience, begins the two-day culture training asking people to chime in by asking this attention-grabbing question: "How many of you know somebody who applied to be in this seat and isn't sitting in this room?" Most hands fly up. Fakhoury explained to me, "We begin the Culture Champion meeting by acknowledging the folks who aren't in the room. We want the attendees to know that they are not the end-all-be-all" and that what matters isn't just being chosen, but "it's what they do after they leave the room as well. And this sense of being better together, and this sense of passing on your learnings to make others more successful" counts in the long run.

Not only does this chiming-in help people wake up and be present in the meeting itself, but it ultimately links them back to their original purpose of being Culture Champions in the first place.

✦ ✦ ✦

At Udemy, the 600-person global learning platform, meetings are a highly ritualized affair where people chime in with an actual pledge to be a "Meeting Hero." A cute graphic is even posted in meeting rooms reminding people. At Udemy, a Meeting Hero is someone who makes sure meetings are necessary, useful, and have an actionable outcome, i.e., have a purpose.

Taking a moment to chime in before meetings and to encourage presence of mind, body, and spirit is just one ritualized part of the Udemy culture. This pause is intentional and aligned with company values, one of which is "Mission-Inspired, Results-Obsessed." Their meetings sure are both of those things! Udemy has achieved "unicorn" status, boasting a valuation of over a billion dollars, and has over 40 million people on its platform. So something tells me Udemy's intentional connecting of rituals and values is paying off.

Still, even with strong rituals like this, it's only reasonable to need some backup. As Shannon Hughes, VP of communications, shared with me, "In each of our meeting rooms . . . our Meeting Hero says, 'Wait, before you leave this meeting, did you achieve the objective, make sure everyone is aligned, and make sure everyone understands the next steps?'" This Meeting Hero is like the trusty Udemy mascot, helping them stick to the Three P's of rituals. In fact, Hughes continued, "Other pieces of meeting hygiene are around making sure that we're being inclusive and getting everyone's input . . . doing the right preparation and having the correct agenda outlined prior to the meeting, so that we're not wasting people's time." Udemy appreciates how important it is to actually stick to their meeting-guns.

A lot of companies set themselves up with a ritual that might or might not be an official protocol, but something people would miss if it disappeared—which is part of my working definition of a ritual. For instance, I talked to Sarah Dowling, LinkedIn's director of learning and development, about her team's thoughtful get-to-know-you chiming-in ritual. And she said,

"It's so funny . . . I just came from a meeting . . . and for the first time we just jumped straight to the business, and I was like, 'That was weird.' "

Chiming Out

In Parker's book, she writes how important it is that we end meetings with just as much intention as we begin. There are various ways to end a meeting well. But they all rely on one important notion. Parker explains, "The first step to closing a gathering well is less practical than it is spiritual or metaphysical: You must, before anything, accept that there is an end. You must accept your gathering's mortality."[22] Sad but true! All good things must come to an end. Using rituals we can end wisely and well.

Avner Mendelson, CEO of Bank Leumi USA, has a valuable ritual that his team hates to miss. Every day he calls a daily huddle for his senior management executives. From 9:30 to 9:45 a.m., these 10 leaders gather for three quick rounds. In the first round, each person shares an update, something as simple as, "I had a great meeting yesterday," or, "I'll be out of the office tomorrow, so don't look for me." Second, they share their "Stucks," something they're stuck on, that perhaps someone in this group can help them with. The idea, to be clear, is not to solve the "Stuck" right then and there, but to acknowledge the need for some assistance, creating accountability. Who wants to be stuck or even to admit they are still stuck on the same thing the following week? The first two rounds are useful and engaging questions, but the closing round, the chiming out, is my favorite. You'll understand why.

The final round of this 15-minute meeting is saved for someone to share a values story, a moment when they've observed an employee living one of Leumi's five values. And, Mendelson told me, "The story doesn't need to be heroic." Heroism is not the point. It could be that someone overheard an employee asking the cleaning staff about their holiday break, a human gesture aligned with Bank Leumi's value of Caring. "This exercise holds the senior team to really understanding the values. They are always on the lookout for clues on where and how they come to life and are celebrated—not just at an annual town hall, but every day." An added bonus is how many of the senior executives have adopted the three-round huddle ritual with their own teams, and each chimes out with a values story. What a perfect transition to the rest of the day.

Another example of chiming out is from Buffer, an all-remote company that helps companies build their brands through social media. Like Basecamp, Buffer's 90-person team, in 19 countries around the world, meets up once a year for a companywide retreat. The purpose of the retreat is to make the in-person connections that only happen through what Carolyn Kopprasch, chief of special projects, calls "condensed kitchen serendipity that co-located teams have."[23] Quite a mouthful, huh? She wants her teams connected.

While there are all kinds of rituals that can help people feel like they belong and connected to purpose even when working remotely, there's just no substitute for in-real-life (IRL), face-to-face interaction.

Over the 10-year history of this exciting, intensive, and exhausting five-day retreat, it has evolved in its intentionality. Like all great rituals, there is a cadence to it, a pulsed rhythm. Monday is a high-energy, all-hands day, focused on reflecting, celebrating, long-term planning, and vision, while Tuesday and Wednesday are for breakout sessions with teams. Then on Wednesday evening, the annual rewards and recognition ceremony occurs. A fun side note on the recognition dinner—"at some point in the night, every other person stands up and switches to another seat so that you can sit next to not only two people but four people throughout the night." Talk about cultivating and curating connection!

Thursday is considered a day off for everyone to be able to explore the destination city with 200 dollars of pocket money. Friday is another all-company day, but it's a lighter day of work. For example, they play a highly competitive game of Team Jeopardy and throw in an "All-Hands Support" initiative for a couple of hours to try to get the inboxes down.

The retreat ends with a gratitude session. Kopprasch gushes, "It might not be an exaggeration to say it's one of my favorite days of the year. It's certainly my favorite moment of retreat."[24] Why? Well, the employees all pass around the mic and talk about things they appreciate about individual people, the company culture, or anything else that comes to mind. On that last evening, instead of everyone hiding out or hitting the bar, the retreat closes with as much intention as it had in the beginning.

But, wait, there's more! Buffer lays claim to what is surely one of the most uncommon, straightforwardly human, appreciative endings of any event I've ever found. The company closes on the Monday after their retreat. Period. What a great way to chime out after a big event, to respect the needs for folks to wind down and digest. They build in a transition day for laundry, jet lag, and reconnecting with family and routines.

Folks, this is ritual at its finest!

In a 2019 *Harvard Business Review* article, Kathryn Heath and Brenda F. Wensil wrote, "Chances are you've attended a meeting today. Was it time well spent or a soul-draining exercise in futility? Although no two meetings are the same, their collective impact on the culture of a company is significant. Meetings matter."[25]

Yes, indeed, they do.

By making sure your meetings have purpose and that those who are in attendance are actually present, your meetings will begin to really matter. And as we know, when people feel psychologically safe and connected to purpose, their performance improves.

As you move forward, consider the little things you already do and see if you might be able to elevate them to rituals status, or see about creating some very simple, repeatable rituals that will remind people of the importance of the Three P's in meetings.

We humans, we love to gather. Rituals make our gatherings matter.

YIELD FOR RITUALS

Meetings of all kinds are here to stay, and rituals can make them more meaningful, purposeful, and fun. This is true whether your meetings are face-to-face or remote. Think about the best meetings you have attended. What made them so good? Were people engaged and connected to each other and the purpose of the meeting, or the question they were trying to solve? How did the meeting begin? How did it end? Was there an opening question or ritual to break the ice or deepen connections? Remember, left to our own devices we're not connecting—even in meetings. Rituals are the tools that can help you transform your meetings from mundane to magical. Give it a shot. What have you got to lose?

RITUALS ROCKSTAR

Priya Parker

Make Purpose Your Bouncer

Priya Parker's Instagram is warm, eclectic, smart, and inviting (as we can see by her 15,000 followers). Like a reflection of her life, she brings together a diverse collection of illustrations, podcast shout-outs ("Dolly Parton's America"), headlines about gatherings, and beautiful photos, not all of herself, but just the right amount to keep us feeling connected. One of my favorite graphics is a simple, sky-blue graphic that says "MAKE PURPOSE YOUR BOUNCER."

She posts great advice for meetings, obviously, and for rituals of every kind, including for our lives.

(continued)

Parker was born in Zimbabwe. She spent her childhood traveling the world with her parents, who divorced and then remarried. Her mother is Indian; her father is from South Dakota. Because Parker spent her childhood "toggling back and forth" between two worlds—one "vegetarian, liberal, incense-filled, Buddhist-Hindu-New Age," and the other "meat-eating, conservative, twice-a-week-churchgoing, evangelical Christian real"—she knows a thing or two about what it takes to keep people together.[26]

Parker understands the importance of ritual.

When I spoke to Parker, she shared a story about a two-day workshop that she facilitated. Every minute of the two days was designed—every session, every transition, every break—everything except the final 10 minutes. "Like a sunset, we assumed [the end] would come," said Parker. When it didn't, after an awkward pause and a "we're done here," the attendees left, but the gaping void lingered.

As human beings, gathering is just something we do. And it's good for us. When we sit together and solve a problem, or get a new idea, or laugh, or move the needle on some big thinking we're doing, it's magic in the extreme. Our feel-goods go up, and our stress goes down.

Looking at Parker's personal life, it's no wonder she became a professional connector—a facilitator and strategic advisor who's worked with pretty much every kind of group and organization under the sun, helping people move away from the same-old, uninspired meeting model to something new and fresh and impactful—something that will truly change the conversation. Maybe even the world.

CHAPTER FOUR

EATINGS

Rituals for the Most Important Meal of the Day: The One We Share

In my favorite research study of all time, the one that inspired the name of my business—the Spaghetti Project—and a new direction in my career, four professors from the Cornell School of Management studied "organizational benefits that firms might obtain through various supports for coworkers to engage in commensality (i.e., eating together)."[1] The professors were inspired to do this research because they saw "that the costs for sponsoring workplace eating—whether . . . for facilities and/or food—[were] clear and easily measured" yet "popular debates about the merits of employer-sponsored eating" . . . were "presently very imbalanced since measures of organizational benefits [were] substantially less clear."[2]

They set out to put an end to any debates, and to prove that eating together is good for business.

The authors first summarized the research from fields such as anthropology and sociology, showing that "communal cooking and eating [are] quintessential human traits . . . [that], most important social events or *rituals* in contemporary societies continue to involve some kind of food"[3] (emphasis mine). They explained how contemporary management research has neglected to study food at work because "the mundane nature of eating can be so easily 'taken for granted.'" They suggested that "perhaps the relatively physical and messy nature of eating . . . is less appetizing [so to speak!] to study when compared with more formal and straightforward managerial topics."[4]

Eating is, after all, so very *human*, or, as the authors point out, "intimate."

Next, they took up the task of showing how "firms can enhance team performance by leveraging the mundane and powerful activity of eating."[5] How might firms transform their everyday routines into workplace magic, you ask?

You guessed it! Through rituals, of course. The best part of every road trip is stopping for lunch, and the rituals roadmap is no exception. The most important meal of every employee's day is the one we share.

These smart researchers wanted to do more than "scratch the surface" regarding worksite eating, so they focused on something very specific and then went deep. They chose to look at cafeterias and other "communal eating locations" that can help "facilitate cooperation" and "enhance team performance,"[6] not unlike the good ol' water cooler. As we know, "much of the important information about how to be successful and productive at a job is not going to be found in a memo or an employee handbook, but rather around the water cooler."[7] Since group cohesion ("how connected your work friends are with each other"[8]) is cultivated via informal workplace socializing, socializing is a key predictor of productivity. A study at MIT showed "workers whose group cohesion was in the top third showed an increase in work productivity of more than 10 percent."[9] Informal gathering around food or drink has proved to be good for business.

The Cornell team's lead author, Kevin Kniffin, is the son of a firefighter, so the researchers decided to study firehouses, which combine a workplace with a cafeteria. Not only would this familial connection give the team an "in" for their visits to 15 firehouses across one city over the course of 15 months, but they recognized that "firefighters have developed a broadly accepted, recognized, and celebrated tradition that coworkers will jointly consume meals that they prepare for themselves." This is true to such an extent that "there exists a subgenre of cookbooks that focus exclusively on recipes generated by firefighters."[10] Cooking and cleaning up is such a part of a firefighter's identity that, in one eulogy quoted in the study, a fallen hero was remembered as someone who "gave you 110 percent whether he was washing dishes or going down a smoky hallway."[11]

Firefighters spend a lot of time in the kitchen and dining room. In fact, "rather than being an isolated part of firefighters' workplaces, the *de facto* dining room in each firehouse was also typically the main gathering location where firefighters could monitor alarms, debrief after returning from alarm calls,"[12] and otherwise be available and ready for action. The firehouse kitchen is so much more than a practical place to cook that the authors interviewed one vegetarian firefighter who made sure to eat his meals at the same time as his meat-eating peers, and even help them clean up.

In order to better understand the relationship between the kitchen and performance, the authors sent questionnaires to almost 400 fire department officers, asking each about the success of their current platoons, compared with others with which they'd worked. They were asked to measure the degree to which people cooked and ate together in their current platoons, as well as about cooperative behavior and job satisfaction.

It turns out that eating together is strongly associated with unit-level performance. Organizations that sit down for a meal together—even without cooking it together—strengthen "social glue." In other words, "the informal tradition of workplace commensality within firefighting units is significantly and positively associated with team performance."[13]

As you think about how to apply this flavorful study to your life at home or at work, consider this: the firehouse meal isn't regulated by the employer. The firehouse meal is not a top-down program, requirement, protocol, or some other official mandate for connection. Rather, this meal takes on a life of its own, drawing on what they refer to as "tacit knowledge," something that can't be forced with a group or team.

In other words—it's a ritual. And, boy, would people miss it if it were gone.

Maybe you're wondering—is a shared meal a ritual that will work for every workplace? Evidently not. According to the authors, elevating the meal to ritual status is only applicable for situations "where cooperation, communication, and organizational citizenship [have] value."[14] Eating together is only important for the kind of workplace that values the Three P's: Psychological safety, a sense of shared Purpose, and increased Performance.

In other words—the human workplace.

Laszlo Bock is the former SVP of people at Google. He turned Google into a place that receives 3 million applications a year, with the chance of getting hired at just 0.2 percent.[15] He's also the author of the thought-provoking book *Work Rules!* and now runs a business called Humu, a people-resources tool used by some of the best and the brightest companies today. Bock is also a big believer in the power of the firehouse meal. He maintains, "We know that trust falls, rope courses, or dramatic sky-diving sessions aren't the key to unlocking real, lasting connections. . . . Research shows that firefighters who prepare and eat meals together are better able to focus and to collaborate on the job than those who don't. To honor this norm, we make it a habit to avoid scheduling meetings over the lunch hour, and to mix up who we sit with each day. Of course, there are always times when we need to go solo for alone time—but we like to think of that as the exception, not the rule."[16] For Humu, eating together is a ritual.

In my work with companies over the past 25 years, I've seen that, sometimes, we need to create and curate connections out of nowhere, and sometimes, we do well to develop rituals and amplify the rituals we already have. As the examples below illustrate, because eating together is the secret sauce to being human, we don't need much help. Most of the time, all we need is an invitation.

Because of the way most of our work lives are structured, the meal most often shared with others is lunch. As a result, you will find more lunch tales than any other sort. But the following stories make clear that breaking bread can happen anywhere and at any time of day.

Breakfast of a Champion

Is it just me, or is there something about the smell of waffles that makes everyone go wild? Maybe it's the hint of vanilla or the flour and egg combo? Or the butter and maple syrup we imagine melting and oozing inside those warm little squares?

When I visited the KIND Snacks office one Wednesday morning last fall, that familiar waffle smell hit me immediately as the elevator doors opened. In the kitchen, I met Neil, whom

Daniel Lubetzky, KIND's founder and executive chairman, had told me all about. Apparently "There are things that happened in [Neil's] life . . . that made him feel very grateful . . . toward KIND and toward the world." So every Wednesday morning, Neil buys all the ingredients and the fixins' and just makes waffles for anyone who wanders in.

The day I visited, Neil made three kinds of waffles: jalapeño, a classic Belgium, and a gluten-free option. It won't come as a big surprise that people show up at work early for Neil's waffles. I watched people move in and out, carrying plates of waffles to their desks, chatting with colleagues as they ate, or sitting at the communal table not because they're required to do so, but because they can't resist the ritual of it.

Another champion of breakfast is Bill Koenigsberg, founder and CEO of Horizon Media, the largest privately held media company in the world with over $8.5 billion in client billings. At Horizon, "business is personal," which might be true for many businesses, but at Horizon, it's stated explicitly. And, Koenigsberg insists, "it's more than a tagline." In Chapter Seven you'll hear more about where that came from (spoiler: Koenigsberg is a rituals rockstar!).

"When I started the company 30 years ago, I talked about building a culture like a family. I had about 12 employees. I brought bagels every Friday. It cost me five bucks back then. I now have 3,000 employees, and I still bring bagels in every Friday. It costs me hundreds and hundreds and hundreds of thousands of dollars in bagels, but that investment of the five dollars has paid off like, billions-fold."

I can't think of a better example of someone who started modestly, worked hard to build rituals with what he had, and watched the payoff grow. And grow. And grow.

Finally, a Free Lunch

It's 10:15 a.m. at Chipotle. Employees have been working since 6 or 7 a.m., chopping tomatoes, making guacamole, shredding the chicken, preparing the line for when the doors open at 10:30. This might seem early for lunch, but sometimes people actually start a-knockin' on the doors as early as 9:00 a.m. At 10:15 a.m., the employees all sit down and eat lunch together. One lucky day I got to sit down with them, too, and get the full taste of the purpose and psychological safety that abounds at this high-performing company.

When I arrived at Chipotle, I was greeted by Garrett Calderwood, a Chipotle team director, who warmly introduced me to Patrick Vasquez, the store manager and the rest of the crew members who were just finishing up the morning prep. The crew refers to the important transition between prep and service as a "grace period," and I could see why. This team was busy but truly graceful, smiling and joking as they prepped. I couldn't wait to get the scoop (of guacamole!). Bringing the team together to eat—on the clock, mind you—perfectly aligns with Chipotle's values, the first of which is "The Line Is the Moment of Truth." The moment of truth is when these employees sit down to enjoy what they're about to serve.

After the bonding, the doors open. This is where the crew members have an opportunity to live their second value—"Details Matter"—by offering to customers everything they've worked on that morning.

Calderwood put it well: "We put a heavy emphasis on people and culture because we know that people are what ultimately make us successful. You can make cars, you can make widgets, you can make burritos, but really it's about people."

Let's hear it for Chipotle!

Of course, not all of Chipotle's 80,000 employees work in one of their 2,500 restaurants. And, since the company's third value is "Authenticity Lives Here," management wanted to recognize that not everyone benefits from the regular restaurant ritual of free lunch. So, that's how Chipotle Day was born. Like in any family, everyone has to be loved equally, to be treated to the same perks. Thus, once a week, at all of Chipotle's corporate locations, lunch is served. There's no formal business agenda—Chipotle Day is just a time to come together and enjoy a meal. On Chipotle Day, people wait for an email to arrive, telling them that the food is ready. They then get up from their desks, and they walk down to the cafeteria to get in line. And here in line, as I've said again and again with rituals, is where so much of the ROI happens. Standing in line, chatting, getting to know each other and building relationships is the magic of the ritual of Chipotle Day. This is where Chipotle's fourth and final value comes alive: "The Movement Is Real."

The Lunch Memo

When Cara Allamano started her new job as the SVP, people, places, and learning at Udemy (the online learning platform we learned about in Chapter Three), she typically worked through lunch and didn't think twice about scheduling meetings between the hours of 12 and 1 p.m. One day, she felt a polite tap on the shoulder from someone who said, "Hey Cara, I don't know if you realize, but you keep putting meetings from 12:00 to 12:30 or 12:00 to 1:00 on people's calendars. And that's when we eat lunch here. We all eat lunch together."

Allamano blushed and apologized. She told me, "I didn't know that lunch was one of those informal—but really formal—rituals that we had here at Udemy that I've come to really appreciate."

She hadn't gotten the memo.

Now that she has, she's a big fan of the relaxed ritual of eating lunch together. She described that feeling she gets, every day, walking into the cafeteria a few minutes before noon, the energy in the air, as some 350 people line up to get food from the free buffet. She told me, "It's a place for us to build connections, to build relationships, to talk about work and talk about not work which I think is really important." When I got there, I could see how right she was. People with trays chatting, walking by us, saying "Hi." Once I saw this ritual myself, I could see why people would be so upset to miss out on it.

Like with the firefighters, what's great about this ritual is that there are no hard-and-fast rules. You don't get dinged if you don't show up, and you can eat wherever you want. Allamano told me, "It's self-regulated. I think it's just one of those rituals from a cultural perspective that has been enduring, and I don't think anything is changing anytime soon. I see new leaders come in where they might be kind of doing their own thing for a little bit, and then, inevitably in a couple of weeks, they're sitting and eating lunch with everybody else."

One thing about the ritual that has changed is that every other Thursday, instead of the lunch buffet being served, Udemy offers what they call "Lunch Roulette." People sign up and are paired with people with whom they don't normally spend much time. The groups go out for lunch—on the company tab.

Allamano told me that while this lunch ritual isn't an explicit part of some kind of good-vibes protocol at Udemy, you can just feel it. As Allamano told me—and I couldn't agree more—"I think that's the beauty of culture, right?"

Better than a free lunch, Udemy is offering magic.

A Pizza Friday Like No Other

Motley Fool, the wild and wacky investment firm founded by brothers David and Tom Gardner (who are our onboarding rituals rockstars from Chapter One) have turned an ordinary pizza day into a ritual to write home about.

On the last Friday of every month, Motley Fool buys 80 pizzas for the office. But what makes this Pizza Friday different from all other Pizza Fridays is that they buy 10 pizzas from eight different beloved pizza joints in the area. Describing how they make it dramatic, Lee Burbage, the chief people officer, tells me, "People are very passionate about their pizza. We open Pizza Friday at noon on the dot. If anyone tries to get pizza at 11:59, it's not there. The line curls around the corner, and at noon everybody floods in. It's chaos because everyone knows the pizza that they want."

On offer are all kinds of pizza, from gluten-free, to vegan, to a Mexican pizza, the most popular from a restaurant just down the street. Once, when the company called to place their order, the Fools were told that the Mexican pizza was no longer being made. After putting up a big fuss and sharing how the Mexican pizza was such a crowd-pleaser, the restaurant agreed to prepare it once a month—only for Motley Fool Pizza Friday. According to Burbage, Pizza Friday is Motley Fool's oldest tradition. And one of the silliest. "There's something about everybody waiting patiently in line and then opening every single box to look—it just makes me laugh."

As Burbage put it, "This is a ritual to the employees. . . . There is no employee survey that would get me that pepperoni preference and be able to deliver that to them."

Which is to say that some rituals are so powerful they go way beyond the details and straight to the heart, as well as the stomach.

Dinner Is the Extra Mile

The human workplace honors relationships. As the firefighters make clear, eating together is a great way to honor relationships. Another way to honor relationships with employees is to show them the door at the end of the day and encourage them to honor their relationships at home to keep their work-life balance in check. But when dinners do happen at work, they, too, can be a place for the Three P's to work their magic.

Slack is a rockstar company for lots of reasons, one of which is that the CEO Stewart Butterfield advocates that people "work hard and go home."[17] But sometimes work dinners are necessary and even the right decision. In those cases, going the extra mile to create an intimate ritual is the way to go. The meal can be a Three P's experience for all. To do this, many CEOs invite teams into their homes for meals, cozy and personal, and separate from the daily work experience. Robert Pasin, the Radio Flyer CEO, for example, throws a catered dinner for his senior team and their significant others once a year that everyone looks forward to. He brings everyone into his home and even gives everyone a special gift. Brian Garish, president of Banfield Pet Hospitals, invites his executives over to his house quarterly. Early on in this ritual, only a few significant others would join. Now, they all come and wouldn't miss it. And he told me that he has trouble getting people to leave at the end of the night!

Another important group of people is a board of directors. Connecting board members over a meal is a good way to ensure the trust and safety they need to make important decisions. I met Amy Chang, SVP and general manager of Cisco Collaboration, at the Fortune Brainstorm Tech conference in Aspen, Colorado. Chang participated on a panel about leadership in the boardroom—a panel where, by sheer coincidence, much time was devoted to board members eating together. The consensus was that, while people may hold back during a three-hour board meeting, allowing for minimal diversity of thought, over a meal people tend to let their guards down. As one of the panelists said, "The best functioning boards do dinner." Chang went on to share a story about a board she recently joined. She reached out to each board member, in advance, for a dinner date before the board meeting in order to get to know them better. She confessed, "I didn't want to disagree with someone for the first time in a public board meeting without first having broken bread."

And then there's Morty Schapiro, the president of Northwestern University, whom we met in Chapter Two. When he was hired in 2009, the trustees let him upgrade the house he was moving into. Built in 1919, the house was lovely, but it had barely been touched. There was no air conditioning, and it couldn't pass fire code. Schapiro said, "The only thing I insisted on is that it had to have a catering kitchen because we were going to do some real entertaining."

He was not kidding!

Ten years and 2,500 people per year later, Schapiro and his wife have hosted over 25,000 people in their home. Talk about sharing a meal!

Schapiro—a truly rituals-obsessed guy—started hosting dinners in his home 20 years ago, when he was at Williams College. He knew how excited the students were to engage with faculty and staff, to mix together at the tables, and he wanted to continue that tradition when he arrived at Northwestern. So, he regularly hosts dinners—sometimes he does a few per week, other times none, like during exams. He's thoughtful and changes it up with the seasons. But there are some things that never change: the caterer, the servers, the time, and the vibe. Schapiro's dinners are something to be relied upon. They're more than just dinners. They're bona fide rituals.

Schapiro explained, "When I think about entertaining, I don't just want to check off the box and have people over. I want them to come over for a meaningful experience. We put undergrad, grad, faculty, and students at each table, and sometimes include some trustees and donors. Every year we have one for the staff advisory council, the faculty senate, and all the tour guides." Schapiro continued, "One of my favorites is we have 19 varsity sports teams, and each coach brings one student, usually a bench player. . . . I'll have someone [from the group coming to dinner] take a shot at the seating plan and the day of the dinner, my wife and I come in and make some last-minute adjustments. For example, if I know that a teacher and student both love music, I seat them next to each other." Because these dinners are so common, many students will be able to attend one at some point in their four years at Northwestern.

At the end of Schapiro's dinners, guests can choose from a huge dessert buffet, with purple take-home boxes. (I'll remind everyone, as a Northwestern grad myself, that purple is the school's color!) Students are urged to fill the boxes with goodies and take them back to their dorms to share with friends. Schapiro delighted in telling me all the details: "A lot of the stuff is dyed purple. So, they're getting purple cheesecake, and they've got purple cookies. They've got purple strawberries. I don't know if that's good for you, but it's part of the thing. We set up this incredible dessert table. We might only have—tonight, for example, it's probably 67 people, and there are probably only 20 undergrads in addition to the faculty, staff, and grad students. But those 20—each take home dessert for 7 people. It's dessert for 140! So, people know every night that I host a dinner because the dorms are always full of desserts."

Feeding people is great. Sharing deserts is generous and thoughtful, but these rituals go above and beyond simple kindness. People would be at a loss without Schapiro's dinners, and I understand why. Schapiro is intentional about the truly authentic message he hopes to convey in this and all of his rituals: "The president is thinking of you." With all that intention and effort at curating connection, Schapiro is a leader after my own heart. Though he has yet to serve spaghetti, his dinners would make the firefighters proud.

The Loss of a Ritual

One of the most powerful aspects of a ritual is how they can help us create a sense of stability. Everything around us is ever changing, and sometimes that change can really sting. But rituals keep us grounded in the present and remind us of our fond past memories. If you're still not convinced about the magic of rituals, consider this next story of a group of real estate agents who went from enjoying a daily, magical, Three P's lunch extravaganza for 16 years to a group of solo lunchers overnight. When Holly Parker started selling real estate at Douglas Elliman, it was January 1998. Leonard Steinberg, who started at the same time, sat next to her, and the two became dear friends. "We bonded because there's so much to know, and there's so much to run around and go see and learn. That turned into just the two of us having lunch together every single day." Every single day—for seven or eight years!

Over time, both Parker and Steinberg added people to their teams. And naturally, their entire teams ate together. Every single day. On some days, certain brokers were running around showing real estate, but someone was always there, holding down the fort for their ritual lunch. Like the firehouse meal, as

Parker told me, "It wasn't an assistant thing." Everyone took turns organizing menus and ordering—that was part of the ritual. We know about the impact rituals have on performance, so it's not surprising that Parker and Steinberg and their colleagues ranked among the most successful agents in the business.

This story went on . . . for 16 years! Then Steinberg left.

Parker felt lost without him.

Afterward, she just couldn't do the lunch thing anymore. Though everyone else on her team still had to eat, as Parker told me, "It felt too hard without him. I just wanted to change everything."

The loss was such a shock to Parker and her team, it was better just to go without lunches for a while. Sure, people continued to sell real estate, but the magic was on hiatus.

After two years, Parker eventually started ordering in again for her team. Lunch still happens every day, with support and story-sharing, but, as Parker acknowledged to me, "It's different. . . . I just do it. I order lunch for everybody."

✦ ✦ YIELD FOR RITUALS ✦ ✦

Mealtime is the ultimate human ritual. We all need to eat, and enjoying food is one of our most primal instincts and pleasures. As far as ritual eating goes, it doesn't matter which meal it is. It can be breakfast, lunch, or dinner, or a snack around the water cooler; what matters is that it's the one you share. Because it doesn't matter when, where, or what you are eating. The ritual of sitting around the table is good for people, great for business, and just might save a life.

RITUALS ROCKSTARS

Firefighters Cook up the Best Rituals

When I began the Spaghetti Project, I became obsessed with firefighters. I reached out to Kevin Kniffin, the lead author of the Cornell study, and we had a long chat over the phone. I looked through archives of firefighters eating together. I read everything I could get my hands on. I took pictures of firefighters when I saw them (once in a hotel I was staying at where we experienced a false alarm and, once, when my kids and their cousins got stuck in our elevator), and I asked them to tell me about their rituals around the table. I gawk from afar when I see firefighters fully suited up in their gear, loading up their cart at the grocery store.

(continued)

RITUALS ROCKSTAR *(continued)*

A friend who knew about my obsession introduced me to Bob Higgins, a career fireman who came from a family of firefighters. We sat down together so I could ask him all my burning questions. I told him about the Cornell study, of course, and I asked him to talk to me about his own experience and thoughts on firefighter performance being linked to meals. Without missing a beat, this is what he said:

"I was having a meal with a bunch of the guys at the firehouse, just shooting the breeze. My buddy Dominick shared with me that when he was younger he was afraid of heights—not what you would guess for a firefighter!"

Higgins admitted that he was kind of surprised as well. But they were chatting, being open and honest, just being themselves.

Only a few hours later, a fire alarm went off. When they arrived at the scene, Higgins remembered what Dominick had shared with him and offered to switch jobs, putting Dominick in a position where a fear of heights wasn't an issue. With that new intel, Higgins was able to be a better and more accommodating team member.

In this case, being a better and more accommodating team member might have, again, saved more lives.

I think about this story all the time, in every context. A real relationship is at the heart of every great decision and outcome. Firefighters get it. Because they're dealing with life and death every day. They're rituals rockstars extraordinaire in my book.

CHAPTER FIVE

RITUALS FOR TAKING PROFESSIONAL DEVELOPMENT PERSONALLY

Spotlight on LinkedIn's InDay

As you know by now, rituals are dear to my heart. And so is professional development. In fact, one of my favorite and most popular chapters from my first book is called "Take Professional Development Personally." In it, I wrote about how the human workplace must move toward creating a more personally compelling and rewarding culture of professional development in order to survive. Employees today, especially millennials and Gen Zers, those who will make up 75 percent of the workforce by 2025,[1] want to grow on the job—up, down, and sideways—and they'll leave if they feel stuck or stagnant. Deloitte's 2019 Global Millennial Survey notes that "49 percent of millennials quit their job within two years" with the top reasons being "unhappiness with compensation, lack of career advancement and lack of professional development opportunities."[2] Since professional and personal development is an important part of every human workplace, this stop on the rituals roadmap is key for keeping professionals fueled up and ready for the long haul.

A sense of being linked to one's personal purpose and human potential is a must-have for people at work, and it's often ranked higher in importance than salary. According to CNBC, "Nearly nine out of ten, or 86 percent, of millennials would consider taking a pay cut to work at a company whose mission and values align with their own."[3] Deep, relevant professional development is where it's at. For many employees today, growing on the job is a must-have, even more important than money. According to data collected by Culture Amp, a company devoted to developing software solutions for workplace culture, learning is more important than compensation. Didier Elzinga, Culture Amp's founder and CEO, explained, "If you have a good manager, it may take them 10 years of experience to become a truly exceptional manager. A company with a strong culture of learning and development can accelerate the process so that manager becomes a great leader in a much shorter space of time."[4]

✦ ✦ ✦

When I was starting out as a consultant, professional development often meant, if you were lucky, you were sent to a conference or maybe a speaker came in for a lunch-and-learn. (Can you remember those days of actually sitting still in a room listening to someone speak without your phone buzzing or ringing for you from your bag? Perhaps not. But I do!). Over time, as technology caught on, online courses became a popular go-to for upskilling.

But conferences, retreats, and other sorts of tried-and-true professional development programs still have their place for sure. In fact, I'm often invited to give a keynote presentation as the kickoff to such events. I like to arrive early, so I can talk to stakeholders to get a truer pulse on the audience to whom I'm about to speak. Of course I always leave plenty of time for questions. I find the time after my talks to be some of the most fruitful, when employees can connect the dots and see how my talk relates to their regular day-to-day. Because for people to learn and develop, the message has to be personal.

The idea that a company can plug a person into a learning opportunity and expect him or her to return educated and ready to execute has been pretty well debunked. Managers and employees would surely agree. In fact, "Only one in four senior managers report that training was critical to business outcomes."[5] And improvement through education and training will be incredibly difficult unless employees feel like they're in a psychologically safe climate.[6] Plus, "If the [organizational] system does not change, it will not support and sustain individual behavior change—indeed, it will set people up to fail."[7]

I've found that cookie-cutter development can be a waste of resources for companies because so little actually resonates for people in this kind of learning experience. People do want to upskill, for sure, and leaders should provide every opportunity for employees to do so. However, employees want more than standard opportunities. They also want to move around the company, be supported in their side hustles, take risks, and go on sabbatical, etc. Leaders who encourage learning opportunities outside a person's "day job" see the bigger picture.

The CEO of a research company I know told me he had paid for one of his most trusted employees to go to graduate school. He shared that he was not surprised when the employee moved on to a different position in another agency. When I asked the CEO how he justified his generosity and overcame the feeling that his employee's departure wasn't "fair," he said he knew she would continue to bring business his way and that he had done the right thing at the time. They had a relationship, and he had honored it. Being willing to support people's personal development is a risk that truly human leaders must be willing to take.

Rituals can help companies find the middle ground, approaching professional development in a way that's engaging, inspiring, and keeps people coming back for more. Rituals can help companies bridge the personal and professional.

LinkedIn InSpires: Happy InDay!

LinkedIn's 16,000 employees take a day off every month for their personal-professional development. And it was something I had to see for myself.

Before my visit to the Empire State Building, the Manhattan home for LinkedIn, I had been in touch with Nawal Fakhoury, LinkedIn's cheerleader/culture champion (in fact, that's her title on her LinkedIn profile). She and I planned to meet during the September InDay, so I could judge for myself. I recall thinking that over email, Fakhoury already seemed so extremely enthusiastic. I couldn't wait to see what they put in the water over there at LinkedIn.

So, on September 20, 2019, I visited LinkedIn to experience InDay, the one day a month when employees can "focus on themselves, the company, and the world. A day to invest, inspire and innovate."[8] I had heard a lot about this daylong employee celebration at LinkedIn, and I wanted to experience it for myself. I really wanted to know: Is InDay a ritual? Just because it happens regularly, would it pass the Three P's test of offering Psychological Safety + Purpose and give a boost in

Performance for the company's 16,000+ employees?[9] Or would it at least pass the test for the 1,000 folks in the Manhattan office where I was going to visit?[10]

I'll admit I was a little skeptical.

The first thing that caught my eye as I stepped off the elevator on the twenty-eighth floor was a poster with LinkedIn's InDay logo. The InDay Logo was surrounded by the 12 icons of the 12 monthly InDay themes: Vision in January, Community in February, Creativity in March, Environment in April, etc. Since I was visiting in September, I was about to experience Wellness InDay. This couldn't have worked out better since I've found that taking professional development personally means bridging learning and wellness. When we ask how we can feel good and connected in our bodies, minds, hearts, and lives, experiencing significant personal learning rises to the top of the list. The opposite holds true, too.

After taking a picture of the sign, I noticed balloons, and then a schedule of events—morning meditation, dance lessons, a health and wellness fair. As I watched inordinately happy-looking people trot by wearing InDay buttons, Fakhoury appeared, smiling, wearing a baseball jersey with LinkedIn emblazoned on the front.

We'd met once before at a conference, and she was just as warm as I remembered.

She led me down the hall to a cozy kitchen space where we could chat before the first InDay event I would attend—a mindfulness workshop—which I was dying to check out. As we walked together, we ran into some of Fakhoury's colleagues who called out, "Happy InDay!" to each other as they passed. I was blown away by all the good cheer at the early hour of 9 a.m., but here's the thing—from the moment I met Fakhoury to the moment I left LinkedIn after lunch—I was smiling, too.

InDay brings with it a variety of options, and people are encouraged to participate in ways that work for them. There's onsite programming on offer all day which employees are welcome to attend as they see fit. Employees can also decide to stay home, like the woman Fakhoury told me about who used the time to finally paint her daughter's room in a unicorn theme for Creativity InDay. I also met people who were pretty much going about their days as usual because they had deadlines, though they said they genuinely absorbed the InDay spirit from the sidelines.

As soon as Fakhoury and I sat down in a little kitchen nook, surrounded by people coming and going for their coffee and snacks, the HR manager in me couldn't help but ask how InDay tracks people's participation. Fakhoury told me, "My first piece of coaching was, we don't police here at LinkedIn. That's not part of our culture. We set guidelines and then we let people act like owners, and we encourage them to do what makes sense."

So while not all employees participate, "what's interesting is [LinkedIn] surveyed employees a few years ago . . . [and asked] 'How much do you value InDay?' Even employees who never participate said, 'I highly value the program, and if you took it away it would send a message that our culture is changing.'"

Right away, I knew we were in serious rituals territory. Remember, while we have the Three P's test for rituals, another way to know if your company meeting or event or lunch or retreat is a ritual is to ask: Would people miss it if it disappeared? Clearly, for InDay, the answer is yes!

It was quickly dawning on me that InDay was encapsulating what professional development *can* be—it's personal, it's flexible, it's rituals-rich.

InDay began in 2010 when just 1,000 employees worked at LinkedIn. The company had been in such "insane hyper growth," Fakhoury recalls, since its founding in 2003, that leaders were worried about burnout. The team searched for ways to keep their talent a number one priority. Then, "The coolest part is that in 2010 we invented InDay, which is short for Investment Day . . . and the individual who came up with the idea and sponsored it was Steve Sordello, our CFO."

Yes, you read that right. The person who came up with the idea of paying employees to improve their lives—once a month—was the chief financial officer! The guy in charge of profit and loss appreciated the value of happy, healthy, human employees. He knew that what we used to think of as soft stuff is actually the new hard stuff, as in hard dollars.

My thoughts were spinning. It seemed the perfect time for some mindfulness.

The "Soft Stuff" Is Really Hard

Fakhoury led me to a room where a mindfulness class for employees was being held, directed me to a seat, and said she'd meet me later in the morning. The session was already under-way, so I felt a little self-conscious squeezing into the room of 17 people around a table. Thankfully and not surprisingly, everyone was pleasant and kind, moving around to make room for me. The course was guided by a leader from wise@work, the developers of an app that helps people learn the "soft" skills needed to succeed at work, one of which is mindfulness.

I often talk about how these days, the "soft stuff is the new hard stuff." What we previously relegated or even disregarded as "people" skills are now front and center as we begin to see how important people's experience at work truly is. In today's complex, demanding workplace, it's more important than ever for everyone to be emotionally intelligent and self-aware. It's not easy! That was never more clear than when I was learning how to sit still for just a few minutes.

Our mindfulness leader asserted that many of us get caught up with things in our minds because we think of them as "per-sistent," "pervasive," and "personal." Then he led us in a meditation, asking us to consider a time when we were anxious about a moment and to see how these three P's (I had to laugh, of course!) were always in play. He wanted us to "give a name to the spiral."

I admit that it was hard for me to sit still, but I had plenty to think about. It was pretty amazing how the silence really did help me feel more settled.

Maybe this is a ritual I should work into my daily schedule, I thought.

Or maybe I'll just stick to Starbucks.

Or maybe . . .

Maybe not . . .

Around and around . . .

Then the time was up.

We took turns sharing our experience. The LinkedIn folks were so earnest and open to sharing their stresses around work situations and how they get caught up in thinking everything is persistent, pervasive, and personal. I was impressed. Many shared how their nervousness felt soothed just by sitting together in silence. Many shared how they felt more focused, just in those few minutes.

Lucky for them, at LinkedIn they can practice mindfulness together every Friday from 9:30 to 10 a.m. What a direct line to psychological safety at work!

Feeling pretty darn open myself, I decided to try the "Git Up Dance Class," so I could get in on the line dance that was taking the world by storm. Being a dancing fool on a Friday morning seemed like a perfectly InDay thing to do.

Git Up!

Someone from the mindfulness class directed me to the Git Up dance space, but I still had a hard time finding it. I realized quickly I was in the right place when I turned a corner and saw three grinning millennials wearing straw cowboy hats, bandanas around their necks, with T-shirts that said Culture Champions, and InDay buttons on their fanny packs. One guy was rocking a full parachute-pant suit.

I was pretty sure I was in the right place.

I entered the studio space where all of the LinkedIn employees were meeting and greeting each other, as they waited for the instructor to arrive.

Maybe you're wondering how on earth learning a line dance can be considered professional development. Mindfulness—

maybe—but dancing? Is this really what Steve Sordello, the CFO who envisioned InDay, had in mind? Maybe he's gone, and his brainchild has spun wildly out of control?

I had already asked Fakhoury this very question and she said, "He's still here. And in very few worlds do you have your chief financial officer encouraging thousands of employees to take time away from their desks, to pause, catch their breath, and invest in themselves."

How does Sordello justify paying employees to meditate and dance? Well, for starters, there's the wellness angle. Mindfulness and exercise are two of the most important ways to stay healthy, happy, and engaged. According to a 2016 survey[11] conducted by Limeade and Quantum Workplace, 88 percent of employees that report as having higher well-being feel engaged at work versus 50 percent of those with lower well-being. What's more, 84 percent of the higher well-being group feel loyal to their teams compared to the 54 percent in the lower well-being group. The findings support that "employees with higher wellbeing are more likely to feel supported by their organization." Since happy, healthy employees are more engaged, more productive, and less likely to leave, the bottom line sees a cumulative benefit.

As I watched people introduce and reintroduce themselves to one another, it dawned on me what an amazing opportunity this dance party was for professional development. More and more we're seeing how impossible it is to be creative at work if we're stuck in a lane—any lane. To create real diversity of thought, reaching out to and hiring all kinds of people is just table stakes. We need to get people out of their silos and bring them together from every corner of the world *and* from within our organizations for meaningful—and fun—opportunities to learn together. The learning doesn't just have to be about Excel spreadsheets or closing a deal or honing your skills as a manager.

Getting physical and being vulnerable enough to do something new is a way to learn how to be a human being, together.

And because the folks at LinkedIn do something like this every month, they're primed for it.

By the time the delightful instructor arrived, people knew each other's names, were sharing laughs, and were ready to partner up. They felt psychologically safe and connected to a purpose. I had to leave to go chat a bit more with Fakhoury, but when I was walking out, I noted for the record that the InDay dancers performance was looking mighty fine!

#InDay

Fakhoury and I found a quiet place to sit right outside of the dance party to talk a little more about rituals at LinkedIn. My initial skepticism was long gone. I was really excited about the morning and eager to chat. By this time, it was clear to me that InDay is not just a ritual but maybe even a prototypical ritual. Not only does it pass the Three P's test with flying colors, but people would lose their minds if it went away. I talked to one woman who had chosen to duck into the wellness fair for just a short bit before heading back to her desk for a deadline. She was chipper-as-could-be, even though she was missing out on the festivities. For her, she said, just knowing InDay exists is enough!

Being absorbed in InDay, I was reminded that an interesting characteristic of rituals is that they have a cadence, a rhythm, a life of their own.

Because InDay happens every month, it shapes life at LinkedIn—there's before InDay, InDay, and after InDay. There's life leading up to InDay, then life coming down and preparing for InDay, like a Friday Shabbat or a birthday or a weekly breakfast. It's a shared marker people and teams use to feel connected to their lives at work. As Christina Hall, LinkedIn's former head of HR, put it, "It's part of the rhythm of the calendar. 'Oh—today is InDay. I don't have to go to that meeting.' It gives the ritual a weight." Hall added that the cadence makes the ritual feel "elevated beyond a perk."

So true! A perk is a discounted gym membership. InDay is much, much more.

Fakhoury emphasized to me, "What's really special is that every employee knows the theme, every employee celebrates InDay at the same point in the month, but they all get to do it wildly differently based on what makes most sense for them."

The InDay ritual is a *personal* take on professional development.

When I asked Fakhoury about other LinkedIn rituals, she shared some great stories about onboarding and meetings. Even with these stories, we kept circling back to InDay. Granted, there were signs everywhere and people walking by, sporting colorful InDay T-shirts. But I began to see how a ritual like InDay can actually give rise to mini-rituals. This is something I've seen catch fire at other companies, too—how a group of people chooses to celebrate its own festivities, often on social media, which is a great use of technology.

Fakhoury shared with me, "I think one of my favorite rituals that I have seen take off over the last few years is that everyone will post on LinkedIn what they did on InDay. So that's a small way to memorialize the ritual, and we have company hashtags that we established five years ago, #InDay and #LinkedInLife."

With a quick scan of the hashtags, I immediately came across a post by an employee exclaiming, "I love that I get to work for a company that invests in my personal and professional development!!"

Fakhoury agrees, "It's a ton of belonging. . . . My favorite part of InDay is actually not the programing that we do, it's waking up on Monday, or right before I go to bed on Friday night, getting on the platform, and my feed is covered with sites across the globe and people across the globe sharing what InDay was for them, and their InDay story.

"The cool thing is, and I think this is where it hits you as an employee, how global this program is. . . . Our culture isn't something that only you are experiencing in the New York office, but something that every single employee is contributing to."

Real rituals create real community.

When Fakhoury and I finished chatting, it was time to attend the wellness fair, before lunch. I checked out the many different vendors offering juices, massages, mindfulness apps, super-stretching, and gym memberships—perks galore. I loved watching the LinkedIn employees peruse the offerings, imagining how powerful it must feel for them to know that their employer has set them up with so much goodness. I wandered over to the cafeteria and struggled to choose between the paella and the seared scallops. I ran into two people who had recently joined LinkedIn from other companies and seemed thrilled by the change. One of the women was in her exercise clothes; she had decided to jog to work, check out the InDay offerings, do a little work, and then jog home. That was her personal, wellness-inspired InDay.

If you've spent time in big organizations like I have, you might still be wondering how LinkedIn pulls InDay off. According to Fakhoury, "Rather than hiring a bunch of people in HR to execute it in 30+ offices, we've got key people like myself in five of our largest global sites. But then we tap these employees who we dub 'Culture Champions.'" who we mention in Chapter Three.

"An amazing example is how in Detroit we've got 60 employees. We've got three main Culture Champions, and today they have planned three different events that almost every single one of the employees is going to end up participating in. . . . I'm not there, but I'm able to support Detroit with a toolkit, with resources, with ideas, a community connection, and then they can say, 'Well what do we want InDay to be this month?' And then they can make it whatever makes the most sense for them and their office. It's a global program with local flare."

In that moment I was struck and tried to summarize with my development hat on: "There's that double layer of professional development. You're investing in yourself, but also these 300 volunteers. Like you said, it's an honor, and they have to apply, but it's a leadership development opportunity."

"Exactly, yeah," Fakhoury confirmed.

The very concept of professional development changes and evolves once we think about the human workplace where the lines between work and life are being redrawn. What makes something "professional" versus "personal?" This is the question we should all be asking ourselves if we aren't already.

One thing is certain. InDay is a ritual that helps people take professional development personally. Everyone can interpret and live InDay in their own way, without pressure or judgment. It's the truly human way to learn.

YIELD FOR RITUALS

Professional development is not what it used to be. It's better! It's personal, and it really, really matters. So take a look at your employee lifecycle and see where you can insert some ritualized opportunities for learning—either with the whole company, in groups, or for individuals. Creating a culture of learning is the human way to go. And it's very good for business.

RITUALS ROCKSTAR

Mindy Grossman

Mindy Grossman, the CEO of WW International (the company formerly known as Weight Watchers), has a personal mantra: "I believe in perpetual self-improvement. I wake up every morning willing to learn and improve."

How does Grossman actualize her lofty mantra? She has a ritual for that!

In keeping with the ol' "put your own oxygen mask on first" philosophy, Grossman knows that in order to lead in developing others, her commitment to her own learning and personal development has to be up to speed first. She describes her ritual like this: "Every week I either allocate time to meet someone, experience something, or expose myself to new ideas. For example,

I was determined to meet Adam Grant after reading his first book, *Give and Take*. We've since become friends. I totally believe in his philosophy of leadership." I recently heard this story recounted on Samantha Ettus and Amy Nelson's *What's Her Story* podcast. Mindy shared that when she reached out to Grant, she said, "I would love to take you out to dinner in St. Pete, and you just wrote a book called *Give and Take*, so you have to say 'yes'—kidding around. And he came!"[12]

And because Grossman is such a DEI (Diversity, Equity, Inclusion) devotee, she makes it a part of her ritual to learn from a diverse group of people. She told me she believes: "Learning comes from everywhere, not just in your area of business. Too many people stay in their limited swim lane. You have to expose yourself across industries, diverse environments, and even sometimes put yourself in a 'discomfort' zone. That's how great ideas percolate . . ."

Study after study show that diversity is linked to all manner of performance—from profitability to value creation, to a higher return on investors' cash.[13] A leader like Grossman, one who uses rituals to take her own development personally, will help the 17,000 employees who work for her take their own development to heart, too.

Finally, in speaking with Grossman, the CEO of a company that inspires healthy habits, I had to ask about her personal wellness rituals. She shared with me how she finds her own wellness by slowing down and staying connected: "This year I set a goal of being even more active and giving myself more 'analog' time! Board games are my family's new passion!"

When we're looking for rituals inspiration, rockstars like Grossman remind us—there's no place like home.

CHAPTER SIX

THE NO-SMOKE BREAK

Rituals for Taking a Breather

Episode 115 of the megahit show *Friends*, circa 1999, is called, "The One Where Rachel Smokes." Jennifer Aniston's character, Rachel, is at her first day of a new job at Ralph Lauren when she realizes that her boss and her colleague head out for a cigarette every time there's an important decision to make. Rachel even gets up the courage and goes outside to try to join them, but they don't want to blow smoke in her face, so to speak, so they move away, leaving her standing awkwardly alone. And totally left out of the loop. Talk about FOMO!

You may not remember the days of the smoke break, inspiring people to gather a few times a day either in a lounge (now I'm really dating myself) or outside, huddling together, offering each other a light, taking one big exhale in unison, then catching up on the latest gossip. But I remember it well. And while I never smoked, I, like Rachel, sometimes wished I had.

Hard to imagine, huh?

Many road trips are long. The best ones leave plenty of time for resting, recharging, and reinvigorating before jumping back on the road. The best workplace journeys are no different, and if you're a lover of taking a much-needed break as I am, you'll enjoy this stop on our rituals roadmap.

According to the director of the MIT Human Dynamics Lab, "Much of the important information about how to be successful and productive at a job is not going to be found in a memo or an employee handbook, but rather around the water cooler."[1] So while we don't need cigarettes for social glue at work, we do benefit from rituals like water coolers. The thing is, those smokers were on a *mission* to get up from their desks. They had a ritual to attend to! We can easily make the same ritual out of drinking water, but instead we often choose to bring our water bottles back to our desk, keeping us tied to our inbox all day, missing out on all the camaraderie and connection—missing out on ritual.

I see this ghost-town vibe all the time when I visit offices—an impressively silent open office filled with people wearing headphones, concentrating. Of course, we need this kind of focus to be productive, but surely not all day and then into the night. We really do need each other to be our best selves. With our urge to compete, and now with our technology making it possible to work all day, every day, combined with the extra pressure of keeping up with the race to inbox zero and social media, our addiction to technology has left us more disconnected than ever. As I often say, left to our own devices—we aren't connecting. That's not good for us, and it's not good for business.

Tony Schwartz is an author and founder and CEO of The Energy Project, a consulting firm that works with people and groups to help them "manage their energy so they can thrive in a world of relentlessly rising demand and complexity."[2] He talks about how when we vary our attention and our activity, we're more alert and engaged. He puts it this way: "You want sprinters. . . . When they're focused, they're really working. When they're resting, they're really resting. They're not in the gray area."[3]

Schwartz argues, "The human body is hard-wired to pulse . . . to operate at our best we *need* to renew our energy at 90-minute intervals—not just physically, *but also mentally and emotionally.*"[4] Taking regular breaks keeps us from getting stagnant, helps us make connections, and gives us the distance to evaluate our goals.[5] It's been proven again and again that "downtime replenishes the brain's stores of attention and motivation, encourages productivity and creativity, and is essential to both achieve our highest levels of performance and simply form stable memories in everyday life."[6] According to a recent Gallup study, employees who experience burnout are 63 percent more likely to call in sick, 23 percent more likely to end up in the ER, and 13 percent less confident in their performance.[7]

Rituals help us pulse our attention, pause, and prevent burnout.

Consider what we've learned about eating as a ritual in Chapter Four, and how important it is to take a break together around the table. In a survey conducted by Tork, a global health and hygiene company, "nearly 90 percent of North American employees claim[ed] that taking a lunch break helps them feel refreshed and ready to get back to work."[8] What's more, the survey found that "81 percent of employees who take a daily lunch break have a strong desire to be an active member in their company."[9] All that is to say, physiologically speaking, our bodies need time to eat, and our brains need time to rest.

But what does "rest" mean in today's always-on world? According to bestselling author Amy Blankson, when employees are taking their well-deserved breaks, they should consider leaving their phones at their desks. In her *Harvard Business Review* piece on "4 Ways to Help Your Team Avoid Digital Distractions," she mentions that "a study of 450 workers in Korea found that individuals who took a short work break without their cell phones felt more vigor and less emotional exhaustion than individuals who toted their cell phones along with them on their breaks, regardless of whether they actually used the phone."[10] Evidently even bringing a phone along gives the break less bang for the buck. Seems crazy, but if we know our phones are available, we'll be thinking about using them instead of truly being in the present moment.

So what are some ways to turn a no-smoke break into a ritual?

When I was writing *Bring Your Human to Work*, I found a great example of a break that really made an impact. Actually! I walked into the Slack Headquarters at 2:50 p.m. on a Thursday to interview someone for the book. I looked around, checked my phone (I know, I know), and waited patiently for my meeting. At 3:00 p.m. on the dot, I heard a loud gong-like noise and practically jumped out of my heels. The next thing I knew, people from different corners of the office started getting up from their desks and parading down the hall. I assumed it was a fire drill and wondered if I should join the line and file out (and, personally, I hoped I'd get to meet a few more firefighters!).

Heart still pounding, I asked the receptionist, who didn't seem to flinch during the commotion, what was going on. She said, "Oh, that's just the gong telling everyone it's time for their 3:00 p.m. cappucino." This was a ritualized caffeine emergency break! I'd come to the right place.

As I joined the crowd, walking toward my own favorite fix, what struck me was the irony that a company like Slack, a company whose bread and butter is people "slacking" each other online, appreciates how important it is to get up and move and connect. They understand the need to "pulse," to add a rhythm to a day or a task, and incorporate the benefits of face-to-face interaction. They even celebrate it with a ritual.

Like the human body's need for a rhythm, our rituals also come to life with cadence. Powerful rituals help us work hard when it's time to work hard and take a break when it's time to back off. It wasn't the nicotine or the tar that made the smoke break so fun and effective. It's that the experience helped people move through their day with pulsed energy, "high" from the oxytocin of connection and from each other, fueled for the solo work ahead. Sometimes we get that boost from a 10-minute break after lunch, other times two weeks on the beach. Either way, ritualizing our breaks helps us pulse our energy so we have more to give.

The No-Smoke Breaks:
Disconnect to Reconnect with Colleagues

In my work as a coach and in my research with companies, I've noticed that people *tend* to like to do quiet, focused work in the mornings—like the Monk Mode Mornings I mentioned in Chapter Two. It's important to get up and take breaks during this kind of quiet work in order to stay fresh and inspired, but these breaks might be pretty short. Then lunch arrives.

After lunch, as deadlines loom and stress spikes, is when people really start to need a no-smoke break—to disconnect in order to reconnect. Doing so transforms ordinary afternoons into workplace magic.

2:00 p.m.: Break with a "Man's (or Woman's) Best Friend"?

Moon Juice is a California-based beauty and wellness brand that uses "plant-sourced alchemy to nourish and elevate body, beauty, and consciousness."[11] Founded in 2011 by Amanda Chantal Bacon (who made it her business—literally—to heal from a hypothyroid condition), Moon Juice is a company on a nonstop mission to create a sustainable, healthy, beautiful world for all of us. And their products—uber pure skincare, supplements, and remedies—go way beyond things to eat or apply. Moon Juice is "a tangible touchstone for a community excited about a new way of living."[12]

So it shouldn't come as a surprise that Moon Juice is a great place to work, one that honors relationships and rituals.

If you follow me on social media, you'll occasionally see pics of my husband and three kids. But some of my favorite and most popular posts are of my dog, Cruiser, who keeps me sane and happy in this crazy working-mom life of mine. So when I talked to Moon Juice, I fell hard for one of their rituals.

When Moon Juice's director of ecommerce was hired, the company agreed to let her bring her dog to work. Now, her pup is the office dog. Every day, around 2 p.m., the dog needs a walk. But here's the thing: when it's dog-walking time, it's not just the dog's owner who gets up and goes for a walk. A colleague or two or three always join in. As Moon Juice president Elizabeth Ashmun said during our interview, "I've never seen her go alone."

I love how this ritual uses something as ordinary and necessary as a dog walk to unleash the team members to get up and move and connect. And what better way to get a jolt of joy than by walking with a best friend?

3:00 p.m.: "We Get Up, We Dance."

As I've mentioned, LinkedIn, IMHO, pretty much gets everything right. In fact, I've yet to see anything in their culture other than gold-star, Three P's home runs.

This story came from a conversation with Sarah Dowling, director of learning and development, and Chrissy Roth-Francis, a senior learning partner, about their 20-person Learning and Development team. But this story is about a different, everyday ritual that came up, and I couldn't resist mentioning it.

Roth-Francis shared with me, "A ritual that I have come to really appreciate is every day at 3 o'clock, we stop what we're doing, and we have a 3 o'clock dance party."

A 3 o'clock dance party? I was in awe, so I asked her how it works.

She continued, "It's one song. There is one person who always takes the lead. She asks for song requests from a different person every day. . . . We get up, we dance. And then we slip back down into our work. . . . It's so ridiculous. We look really silly to everybody walking by. But it's something we can count on."

Something they can count on? Remember the mark of a true ritual? These people would definitely miss their dance party if it disappeared.

As Roth-Francis said, "It shocks me because every day it happens, and I'm like, 'We're still doing this.' Even the most introverted of the group will be doing some kind of dance move at 3 o'clock."

I had my ideas about what made this such an important way to break up the day, but Roth-Francis said it best: "To me, the impact is we're all working by ourselves at our computers, and then 3 o'clock comes, and she just starts playing the music, and suddenly, we go from being individuals to being part of a team."

4 p.m.: Push-Ups at Allbirds

Allbirds is the super-cool, super-successful footwear startup that makes shoes out of merino wool and ships them around the world—including to those in need—in 90 percent recycled packaging.[13] If this sounds impressive, just wait: They're valued at $1.4 billion.[14] And they're a B-Corp, a company where giving back is baked into the business. So, what gives!? They do!

Meet Tim Brown, Allbirds cofounder, native of New Zealand, home of the Haka dance from Chapter One, and captain of the national soccer team, who led his team to victory around the world.[15]

Growing up around sheep, Brown began to wonder why their wool, being so sustainable, wasn't being used in shoes. Eventually he met Joey Zwillinger, an engineer and renewables expert, and together they came up with a type of wool that could be used specifically for footwear. The next thing that happened was "an entirely new category of shoes inspired by natural materials, and an ongoing mantra to create better things in a better way."[16]

Brown's days on the soccer field taught him a thing or two about team building. And inspired a bit of athleticism in the office. Enter: 40 at 4. Zwillinger shared with me, "One of our very early employees found himself feeling weak. His friend challenged him to do 2,000 push-ups before the end of the year, and he calculated that he would need to do 40 of them every day to meet his goal. So he started involving the whole company in it, and that became 40 at 4. Forty pushups at 4 p.m. There was no rhyme or reason. It just organically became a ritual."

Maybe no rhyme or reason, but this break-time ritual definitely has a rhythm—a cadence.

The 40 at 4 is led by a different person each week, who also gets to add a lesson in their own favorite activity—from Pakistani dancing, to a crystal sound bath, to cricket.

"It's a really cool way to break up the afternoon at that natural low point of your day."

And it's way healthier than smoking, an overload of caffeine, or dipping your hand into the candy jar.

Don't Even Try to Stop the Madness

Another great way to create rituals that really mean something to people is to ride on the coattails of what's already happening in the office, especially if it's grabbing everyone's attention. Embracing cultural events, for example, is a powerful way for companies to gather together and bask in the glow of connection. I've met some shortsighted managers over the years who complain about lost productivity and how "no work gets done" during events such as the World Cup and the World Series. These are often the same people who on another day spend ridiculous amounts of money trying to increase employee engagement.

They don't understand how to turn a distraction into a ritual.

Take March Madness, the adrenaline-inducing, beloved basketball tournament. According to the Chicago-based outplacement firm Challenger, Gray & Christmas, the projected cost of March Madness, due to lost productivity is "nearly 13.3 billion." That's some serious cash. But "trying to ban March Madness activities from the workplace would cost employers far more in employee morale, camaraderie, and culture, which is particularly important when the labor market is really tight, and companies are fighting to retain and attract the best people."[17]

That's where rituals come in.

ZogSports is a 650-person company that connects people through their shared love of sports via leagues, tournaments, and other fun activities. During March Madness everyone who works at ZogSports goes bananas, so founder and CEO Rob Herzog decided to just go with it. He told me, "We close the office at 12:15 p.m. on the Thursday March Madness starts, and all 28 NYC HQ employees go to a bar to watch together. We run two March Madness pools—one for our full-time staff and the other for both our field team and full-time staff to build connections and community around the tournament. We also let people stream games if they want when the office is open." Herzog doesn't see the time away from the office as a loss, but as an oxytocin-fueled break. It's a Three P's win for everyone.

Sports aren't the only cultural events that can draw people's attention away from work or so-called "productivity." At Microsoft in Redmond, Washington, home to almost 40,000

Microsoft employees,[18] Halloween has taken on supernatural proportions.

Instead of people with small kids ducking out early for Halloween parades and to prepare for trick or treating, Microsoft invites spouses to load up the minivans with kids in costumes and descend on the campus in the afternoon. People decorate, give out candy—the whole nine yards. When I talked to Irada Sadykhova, senior director of organization development at Microsoft, she told me, "If you want to get home without sitting in traffic for three hours, you better get out of here before 2:00 p.m., because after 2:00 p.m. it's impossible to get out of campus."

Sadykhova has been at Microsoft for over 15 years, so she's seen all kinds of zany rituals. And while the company has matured, they still love Halloween because it's a time when the working parents can trick or treat at work. The best part is that this Halloween ritual, which has been around for decades by now, was never actually instigated by anyone in particular. As is true for many rituals, it just happened. "We don't promote it necessarily, but it's the thing that people treasure."

While much has changed at Microsoft, as Sadykhova said, "Please don't take away Halloween."

Disconnect to Reconnect with Family and Friends

The key to any successful enterprise, according to our friend Tony Schwartz, CEO of The Energy Project, is not building people's skills or knowledge base as we often think. It's learning how to manage people's energy. So much so that Schwartz thinks "CEO" should stand for chief energy officer. Good CEOs know that everyone's better off with well-rested, well-pulsed employees who are connected to colleagues, friends, families, and to themselves. What better way to make sure employees are energized than to encourage them to get away from work for an extended period of time and truly disconnect in order to reconnect? Smart companies know that we need to do good work and get away. But in this work-addicted world of ours, how do we do it? How can we shift the culture in our own companies to align with human goals with more meaning than staying on top of our inboxes?

Rituals can help entire companies support good and real disconnection. In a 2016 study conducted by The Energy Project and Zogby International, approximately 30 percent of the respondents who affirmed the statement *I am comfortable taking renewal breaks during the day* reported being "more focused, engaged, committed to their work, and likely to stay at the company than those who weren't comfortable with renewal breaks."[19]

In addition to during-the-day breaks, another approach is to make a ritual out of vacations. In order to encourage employees to take time off to recharge, the award-winning digital community Food52 closes its offices for two weeks a year. This is how it's described in the handbook: "Summer Week was invented in the early days of Food52 because we wanted to take a tip from the Europe playbook, and take a civilized summer break. It also happens that many of the projects we work on through the year are for Q4, so it's a great time to take a breather, cool your jets, see family and friends, or just go for a swim before the fun and thrill of the holidays are upon us."

They also provide a platform for employees to share what they did over the week, which is often food-related.

> I spent most of the week cooking the recipes I had wanted to make all summer but never got around to— like Virginia Willis' deviled eggs.
>
> —SARAH

> The brown butter peach pie I made in the middle of the day, IN THE MIDDLE OF THE WEEK, to procrastinate hanging some shelves. Worth it.
>
> —KENZI[20]

Sometimes it's just easier to close up shop than to manage the resistance and vacation schedules. Other times, closing on a certain day is a ritual that makes a statement. Similar to Food52, LinkedIn shuts down for a week over the Fourth of July, and since 2014, outdoor and adventure retailer REI has closed all of its stores on Black Friday while paying employees during the time off. According to an article in *Business Insider*, CEO Jerry Stritzke (who resigned in 2020) set out to make his radical move in order to " 'put a stake in the ground' and make a statement against the growing trend of retailers kicking off their holiday sales on Thanksgiving Day." He said, "I was looking at the chaos of Black Friday and how more and more stores were opening on Thanksgiving, and it just didn't feel right." But Stritzke didn't stop there. Instead of encouraging shopping or working, he turned Black Friday into a day for people to #OptOutside and #OptToAct, encouraging employees to get outside and clean up the climate mess we've made. "#OptOutside began as a moment that turned into a movement. Now it's a mission—that's why we're equipping everyone to act."[21]

In my first book I talked about sustainability being one of the key components of a human workplace. There is nothing more human than making a ritual out of being sustainable. What's more, REI is an outdoor sports company, so getting outside and being in nature is a part of what they do. So this ritual taps right into their values! REI is leading the charge on sustainable business practices that keep us all in business, if you know what I mean.[22]

In 2019, I happened to hear Jen Lindenauer, director of local brand engagement at REI, speak on a panel at the Riveter Summit in New York City. Lindenauer talked about how crazy she initially found it for a store that makes its money from retail to close on the busiest shopping day of the year and how the idea originally came from the head of merchandising, someone who clearly has a vested interest in that day. But now, as the person in charge of the brand, she said, "It makes my job easy. . . . I have a brand where people know we care."

Rituals That Remind Us: You're Not All That

The investment firm Motley Fool has an interesting approach to just about everything, and the company's vacation rituals are no exception. Unlike many companies where people have to be forced to take a vacation, people at Motley Fool (where there's an open-ended vacation policy) tend to take up to four weeks a year. This would be good enough for most companies, but not for the folks at Motley Fool. They don't just want people to go on vacations in order to refresh, recharge, and reconnect. They have a crazy ritual at the monthly All-Hands meeting where they pick one person's name out of a hat to go on a two-week vacation with zero contact with the company. The chosen one must take the two weeks off before the next All-Hands. Motley Fool even contributes 1,500 dollars to support the fun, and then the employee has to share what they did.

Why does the vacation have to be immediate, you might ask? What's the point of what might seem like a fool's errand ritual?

According to Lee Burbage, Motley Fool's chief people officer: "It's linked to the company value of being collaborative. . . . You're forced to be collaborative if a key team member leaves. No one person is indispensable."

What a lesson in letting go!

He continued, "It's our continued push to try to make sure people understand that if you take breaks, you will be happier and a better employee, and it's better for our business, right? So if you think you're being the hero by working all the time, that is false."

One of my favorite stories that comes from the Motley Fool's nobody-is-indispensable lottery is when they had just hired a new president. Lo and behold his name was picked out of the hat to take an immediate break. The company was in the midst of launching a new product line, and the new president assumed there was no way he would go away on a break. Right? Oh, how very wrong he was. According to Burbage, the president looked at him and said, "This is not for me, right? I'm the president. And I just started." Burbage responded, "That was funny. . . . no one person is indispensable."

So, off he went. Not so foolish, after all.

YIELD FOR RITUALS

We're often working all day long. Breaks help us maintain our energy and connection, but without intention, they might not happen. So think about how you and your employees spend your days and look for opportunities for ritualized breaks along the way.

RITUALS ROCKSTAR

Aimée Woodall

Aimée Woodall Takes Us All to Magic Camp

One day I got a mysterious package in the mail. I opened it up and saw a gold sheep trophy with the words, "Fu*k Yeah" emblazoned on the bottom. I thought to myself, "What on earth is this?"

And then I opened the enclosed card.

Dear Erica,

I recently read *Bring Your Human to Work* and was so inspired. You articulated so many things our agency practices and I loved reading it. We're celebrating our tenth year in business with a series of "Fu*k Yeah"

(continued)

RITUALS ROCKSTAR *(continued)*

trophies sent to people we admire. It's a tradition we practice internally and now we're sharing the admiration. Thank you for all you do . . .

The letter was signed from "Jess and the Black Sheep Team."

I didn't know Jess, and I'd never heard of Black Sheep. On the back of the card was Jess's email, so of course I wrote right away to thank her for both her kind words and the awesome trophy! And that's how I learned about and eventually met Aimée Woodall, Black Sheep founder, CEO, and chief strategist of the Houston-based "brand strategy and creative agency that wakes up every day with the goal of activating people around things that matter."[23] (I also got to meet Jess, "office meteorologist, keeper of minutes, lover of jean jackets, master of Post-its.")

I learned about the origin of this amazing Three P's ritual and also learned a lot more about other incredible rituals they have all over their company roadmap.

One of my favorites is called "Field Day," and it's how Woodall helps her company of 18 take a much-needed break from their work. As she told me, it's a "multipurpose thing where we're killing a few birds with one stone, so to speak."

Every six weeks, the group takes a full day off—together—outside of the office, exploring their hometown, poking around in new neighborhoods or institutions they're not familiar with. This is so important because they're intentionally taking a break from the day-to-day that we know full well tends to suck us in.

While upping their own game as a team, they also consider what's happening with clients and take the time to "now talk about [particular projects] with everybody in a way where everyone can contribute their perspective and insight."

Because Woodall's such a rockstar, she doesn't just know how to take a break; she knows how to purposefully gather her gang as well.

Twice a year, the entire team goes away for a three-day retreat—once in the summer and once in the winter. "Jess always puts together this quick review of the year, which is mind-blowing every time I see how many things we moved forward, and to see it all in one place. The rest of the time is all about reconnecting to what is important and what we all want to build. There is a strong sense of every voice at that table and really wanting to have an agency where what everybody wants to be doing is talked about, and then we find patterns within that and things to really tackle together in the new year."

Woodall gets it. She understands the power of ritual to help pulse her team's attention and energy, even though, as she admits, "It's always hard because there is so much to be done to take [time away from], but we never regret it when we do. . . . It really enriches everything that we do thereafter and makes us more efficient when we get back anyway."

Woodall also gets that it's nothing crazy or unusual to take her team away for a retreat. In fact, it's perfectly ordinary. Which makes it all the more fantastic that she calls these retreats "Magic Camp."

CHAPTER SEVEN

WE SEE YOU

Rituals for Recognizing and Rewarding

Millennials and Gen Zers have brought many things to the table that we all need. One of those things is an insistence on being recognized at work—for a job well done, for sure, but also feedback about what's working and what isn't. Ideally, feedback happens all year round, and not just once a year at review time. In one study, 60 percent of Gen Zers reported that they want "multiple check-ins from their manager during the week; of those, 40 percent want the interaction with their boss to be daily or several times each day."[1] And in a 2018 survey from EY, a global professional services firm, "Largely all of Gen Z (97 percent) is receptive to receiving feedback on an ongoing basis or after completing a large project or task, and 63 percent of respondents prefer to receive timely constructive feedback throughout the year."[2] The numbers are in. People want feedback about their work and a lot of it!

But that's not all they crave.

Feedback is great, but younger workers have upped the ante by asking to be recognized simply for actually being participants, for being real, live human beings in the room, and not just cogs in the corporate wheel. Imagine! Though we think of these young workers as obsessed with digital communication, actually "72 percent of Generation Z want to communicate face-to-face at work."[3] Even an entirely digitally native generation craves that human connection. Millennials want feedback. Fifty percent more than their other coworkers, in fact.[4]

I often hear grumblings about this desire for constant feedback from older people, going on about how their younger office mates are "needy," or—the insult millennials get most often—"entitled." Remember that 2013 "Me Me Me Generation" *TIME* magazine cover? The first line of the subheading read, "Millennials are lazy, entitled narcissists who still live with their parents."[5] I don't see it that way.

Of course, any strength can become a weakness when it's out of balance, but the truth is that if wanting to be seen means we're needy, then count us all in. Being recognized is just after food and water in the hierarchy of human needs. Think about it—shunning someone is one of the cruelest forms of punishment, and showering someone with the sunshine of our sincere attention is the highest compliment. At this stop on the roadmap, I'll share ways of celebrating that make everyone shine.

A client shared a story of an exit interview that she had with a top-performing employee at an investment bank—an employee that both she and the firm really didn't want to lose. The employee shared that the reason she recently left her company wasn't that she didn't enjoy the work or the hours or her colleagues. It was just, "I felt like my manager didn't see me." Wow.

I know this can feel like a lot. On top of everything else you're expected to do at work, you have to "see them"? Now, we have to consider people's feelings?

Well, yes.

So much of what it takes to succeed in the human workplace is this basic. Though it's not rocket science, it definitely isn't easy. In today's workplace, the soft stuff can sometimes feel like the hard stuff, and it can be challenging to figure out how to squeeze it all in.

But have no fear—rituals are here.

Next you will see three ways that rituals can help people feel seen, appreciated, and that they belong. We've seen in previous chapters that when rituals are tied to a company's values, they're extra magical because they also help people feel tied to purpose. Because remember . . .

Psychological safety + Purpose = Performance.

Here are three different kinds of rituals that can send the message *We see you*: (1) rituals that reward individual performance, (2) rituals that reflect milestones, and (3) rituals that connect to the collective.

And the Winner Is: Rituals That Reward

There's nothing new or particularly magical about companies handing out annual awards. What makes some of these events rituals, while the rest remain simply a part of regular corporate programming?

Let's return to the indicators of what makes something a ritual. First, people miss it when it's gone. That's a nonnegotiable. Second, it rises above and beyond its practical, operational use. Lighting a candle isn't necessarily a ritual. But it is if it's done in a very specific way, for a reason other than to provide light or freshen up the room. In other words, a ritual *means* something. And third, a ritual must pass the Three P's test. Does the award or event help people feel Psychologically safe, and is it linked to a Purpose, ultimately boosting their Performance?

A ritual may also live on beyond the person who came up with it. Do you remember the stuffed penguin ritual from the company DoSomething? A *former* employee had the penguin on his desk and just started passing it around. That person has since left the company, but the passing of the penguin is one of the company's most sacred rituals.

A Very Sh*tty Award

In the fall of 2018, a Ketchum PR manager found herself with a team of fresh, bicoastal talent assembled to work on an important toy account. Most of these young marketers and influencers were both new to the company and new to the product. The team was "phenomenal," yet as is typical of many young people (and women especially), they were hesitant to "brag" or toot their own horn. Their leader—let's call her Leslie—knew how important it was for people to be recognized and celebrated. So she took it upon herself to make it happen. First, Leslie implemented a Person of the Month award that she presented to an outstanding member of the team. Nothing wrong with that.

But Leslie also wanted to encourage more reflection and more collaboration. "I knew I wanted to do team awards but just wasn't sure what I wanted the award to be. I was going through a bunch of different trophies on Amazon and saw the toilet. At first I thought, 'How strange is this?' But then I realized we had a lot of sh*tty things happen recently, but the team had pushed through. Best $14.99 I ever spent!" Leslie came up with the idea of awarding a golden toilet to the person on the team who had the "sh*ttiest moment" (Yes! That's the real name of the award!) and turned it around, with the help of the team, of course! The award was an instant hit with people who had had to deal with a difficult account or a last-minute all-nighter. Leslie chose and awarded the first golden toilet, and then the first winner awarded the next, and so on.

An unforeseen bonus of this award is the fact that it sits on someone's desk, inspiring conversation from bypassers. What could be better than office chat about how to improve on our worst moments with our team?

The Sh*ttiest Moment Award was such a big hit that it truly shifted the culture of Leslie's teams (and other managers were inspired too!) to one where everyone sought transformative experiences and opportunities to help each other. One where peer recognition could be just as important—if not more important—as being recognized by Leslie herself.

When I asked Leslie if the golden toilet will outlast her, she said she thinks so. "I don't even know where the toilet is at this point." From a rituals point of view, that's exactly what you want. The ritual has taken on a life of its own.

Rewarding Kind Customers

If you ever see a man on the street or in an airport doling out KIND bars from his backpack, don't worry. That's just Daniel Lubetzky, founder and executive chairman of KIND Snacks, philanthropist, Shark Tank entrepreneur, and lifelong devotee of being, well, in a word—kind. He doesn't just recognize his employees through ritual, but he pays attention to his customers, too. And kindness is always at the heart of it.

Early on, Lubetzky launched a ritual and called it KINDOS, recognizing employees and rewarding them with KIND bars and cards of gratitude. He now has a long-standing tradition of awarding one employee every year with a KINDOS award.

One day, November 13, 2015, World Kindness Day, the internal KINDOS ritual went viral when they launched the #kindawesome campaign for the digital world. This public ritual charged fans and followers to call out acts of kindness throughout their lives and post them to social media. In its heyday, this campaign identified over 300,000 acts of kindness.

I asked Rachel Warncke, an office coordinator in Manhattan, if she had ever handed out one of the company's #kindawesome cards to a stranger (which entitle the person to free KIND bars). She shared a story of thanking a man who had given up his seat on the subway for someone who needed it, then handed him a card. I asked Warncke how it felt, and her face lit up as she said, "Awesome!"

Though the #kindawesome cards have come to an end as a public campaign, Lubetzky continues to recognize kindness. Lubetzky told me, "So when I travel on a flight, I always bring 72 KIND bars, and I hand them out." Why 72? Each box has 12 bars in it, and six is the number of boxes he can carry with him. Think about how seen these people feel when Lubetzky recognizes and rewards people for random acts of kindness from a brand that now has mass recognition itself. Through this ritual, the ordinary KIND bar becomes something else, something that connects people to Lubetzky's purpose of being kind.

A Next Level Celebration

On a hot summer day in August 2019, I popped into a bustling event space in lower Manhattan, a space filled with hundreds of chatty, vibrant people moving toward the chairs sitting in front of a stage. While everyone was friendly enough, I was a little uncomfortable, which makes perfect sense. This was the Avenger's Ceremony, an extraordinary ritual on the most exciting day of the year for the Next Jump community. The day was not designed to keep *me* feeling connected. In fact, that I felt like an outsider is a great indication of how strong the Next Jump culture is.

Next Jump is a 2-billion-dollar e-commerce platform for jump-starting workplace culture.[6] The company's work touches 30 million employees each year, across Fortune 1,000 companies. Moreover, Next Jump reinvests in its mission: "We use the revenue generated from this platform to fuel our social movement: Changing workplace culture."[7] Would you think a values-driven company like this has rituals? You bet!

I had the pleasure of being invited to the Avenger's Ceremony, the annual gathering to recognize that year's Avenger, a Next Jump employee who "embodies what it means to be a steward leader." The award goes to one person from their team of 200: "They do the little things to enable you to do the bigger things you are meant to do. A person who is not only committed to bettering oneself but also constantly believing in your potential by holding you to a higher standard. An Avenger is someone who supports you through the ups and downs, professionally or personally, and is always there when you need help."[8]

Fittingly, the ceremony began with a keynote by one of my heroes, Amy Edmondson, the Harvard Business School professor whose work focuses on the importance of psychological safety. Of course, I took copious notes.

After Edmondson came the presentation of the most esteemed award in the company. The biggest stunner of this ritual is the way families are included. The winner's family is flown in from wherever they are in the world, an incredibly generous gesture on its own. But get this, the families of the two runners up are also flown in. All of the families have to be there because the winner is announced live and in person.

So, all these families were up on the stage while founder and co-CEO Charlie Kim gave an inspiring talk about the prior years' winners. Some of these past Avengers then spoke about each of this year's candidates in such a loving way that I could appreciate how well these team members really get to know one another.

When it was time to announce this year's winner—Graham Laming from Next Jump's London office—we met his dad in person but learned that his mom is afraid of flying. She and Graham's grandparents were projected from the United Kingdom onto a big screen via a video conferencing app.

You might be asking what the award actually is, if all this pomp and circumstance is worth the wait. Let me tell you, it is!

The award is a $50,000 vacation package to share with their family. That's a no-joke award of recognition from Next Jump to one lucky and deserving Avenger. From the beginning to the end, this ritual is tied to Next Jump's mission of "Better Me + Better You = Better Us." Who wouldn't want to feel like they belong to such a purpose-driven company?

Attagirl for All

People like to win prizes. Who doesn't love the bragging rights of a golden toilet or an all-expense paid trip? But rituals that recognize don't have to be glamorous or offer a prize to make an impact and have meaning. One of my all-time favorites is simple, authentic, and doesn't cost a thing.

Shanna Hocking, associate VP of development at the Children's Hospital in Philadelphia, shared a ritual from her time as a college intern at the Duke University development office. Her mentor approached her with a manila folder and said, "This is your 'Attagirl Folder.'" Hocking confessed, "I'd never even heard the expression 'attagirl.'"

Her mentor explained, "You need to fill it with all of your accolades, all the notes you get, all of your accomplishments. . . . This is going to be the cheerleader that you need on days when things don't go the way you've planned, or you're feeling unsure. This is going to remind you of how amazing you are."

Hocking told me, "I have kept that folder with me throughout my entire career."

Now that Hocking is a leader herself, she ritualistically gives a plain folder to everyone who starts to work with her. "And I tell them exactly what was told to me. I tell them how it was told to me, because I want them to know that they're part of this tradition. And then I tell them that it's my job to help them fill the folder."

How does she help them stick to this ritual? She keeps her own email file and collects all the great work they're doing to share with them. It's a ritual for Hocking, too.

When I asked her if the guys on her team get an "Attagirl folder" too, she said everyone can name their "Attagirl folder" however they wish. Support does not discriminate.

Rewarding people is a well-worn method to keep people motivated and engaged, but turning rewards into rituals goes a step in a more human direction by helping them feel supported and connected at the same time.

We See You: Rituals That Reflect Milestones

We spend an awful lot of time at work, and we need to feel seen while we're there. Put simply, we want our presence to be reflected back to us. Rituals are an incredibly efficient way to give people the boost of being seen and appreciated without a lot of complicated or expensive programming. In this section I will share some rituals that reflect milestones that occur when we just keep showing up. Really, what's being celebrated and reflected is a person's presence. You might be surprised how powerful the smallest of gestures can be.

Design Your Own Adventure

Our Chapter Six rituals rockstar, Aimée Woodall, asks people to create their own adventure on their first anniversary at the Houston-based marketing, strategy, and design agency, Black Sheep. She and her team know how tough the first year can be, so they really go all out and take the entire 18-person company out for an evening "crafted around who they are, what they care about, what they like, and their personality."

Um. Wow!

As Woodall told me, "It might be a very extravagant dinner, especially if they are a foodie. For some people, it's like I want to go get hot dogs and go to the Astros game. The greatest example of a totally different approach was when we brought picnic lunches and went to a bingo hall because that's what that person wanted to do."

Black Sheep, being the ones on the outside of the herd, have an interesting take on what it means to belong. They certainly know how to create a ritual that makes a lifelong impression! Making a ritual personal ensures that it won't be forgotten.

The Cookie Jar at DICK'S Sporting Goods

DICK'S Sporting Goods was founded in Binghamton, New York, in 1948 when Dick Stack's grandmother asked him how much it would take to buy enough merchandise to pursue his dream of having his own bait and tackle store. His answer was $300, and his grandmother, a woman from the Depression era, reached into her cookie jar and handed over $300 in cash.

DICK'S, the company, has turned this personal story into a ritual. At DICK'S, the cookie jar is a big deal and signifies true commitment.

When people have been at the company for 20 years, they get a personalized DICK'S Sporting Goods cookie jar with $300 in it. This may not seem like much, but the money isn't the point; it's the direct tie-in to Dick's story and purpose that matters. And besides, it's actually $350 they receive so that after taxes it's $300. Some things never change. Paying taxes is one of them.

What a clever way to help people invest in a company. When even the smallest financial reward is tied to a company's story, the award recipient will become part of history.

Microsoft M&M's

Microsoft is arguably one of the most serious companies on earth, but they have quite a history of being pranksters in the office. I'm a big fan of sweets, so I love their over-the-top anniversary ritual.

In addition to the more traditional award for service, Microsoft has a ritual where employees bring in a pound of M&M's for every year that they've worked at the company on their work anniversary. This tradition dates back to the 1990s when one of the teams celebrated the tenth anniversary of a few of its members by buying 10 pounds of M&M's at the local Costco.

Today we're not just talking about a bag or two. Microsoft's been around a long time, as have its employees, so there are 20-, 25-, and 30-year anniversaries. As Irada Sadykhova, director of organization development at Microsoft told me, "Somebody had 20 pounds—that was a moving crate!"

Even one of the most serious companies in the world makes it their business to have fun. Rituals remind us how important it is to take the time to have a good time—together.

Put Your Rituals in Writing

The ease and accessibility of emailing and texting has made letter writing a cherished form of communication. When we modern folks take the time to sit down and write a letter, it says a lot more than whatever it is we've written—it broadcasts that we care. Leaders from all kinds of companies take advantage of this automatic "we see you and we care" immediacy of letter writing and have made rituals out of it.

Here are just a couple:

- When Bill Koenigsburg started Horizon Media in 1989, he wrote to his few employees on their anniversary with the company, something along the lines of, "Thank you so much for what you do!" This was a general form letter, but he always made sure to handwrite a personal note, with his signature. Fast-forward to 2020, and Koenigsberg tells me, "Today I write 3,000 anniversary notes annually, and if someone doesn't get one for whatever reason, I get a call saying, 'Where's my anniversary note?'"

    The card itself is just the first part of the ritual. Koenigsberg is quite particular about his pens, and he only writes in green. "It's the only color pen I'll use. And I have green folders. Green is a sign of good luck. It's a sign of money. If any red pen ever comes near me, I break out in hives because in business red is loss."

    By the sound of it, his passion for rituals has spread throughout the company. "This year [2019], we celebrated our 30-year anniversary at Horizon, and the employees provided me with my own 30-year anniversary note. It was a book personalized from 3,000 employees writing to me the same way I write a happy anniversary note. Each of them was written in green . . . which is pretty special."

What a great reminder that it's not just the youngsters who want to feel seen.

- Daniel Lubetzky, KIND's founder and executive chairman, has a similar ritual. "I personally email team members when it's their birthday and anniversary at KIND. We have 700 people, so that's like 1,400 emails a year, right? It's not a little work, but it means a lot to people." It sure does!

But, wait, there's more. Lubetzky shared with me, "When people have monumental anniversaries (fifth, tenth, fifteenth), they get a little gift from us. When employees' kids are born, we send out an announcement and send the employee a onesie with a 'KIND MINI,' (a bar that's half the size) logo on it. The family takes photos of the baby, and we include them in our newsletters." What a kind, engaging ritual to keep new parents feeling that they still belong and are valued.

Mustache Day!

Celebrating birthdays and anniversaries is a wonderful age-old ritual that's almost as common in companies as in families. Just like at home, lots of companies personalize these rituals to reflect their family style. The more personal they are, the more Three P's–effective they can be, helping people feel like they belong to a very specific, connected group.

Jellyvision, the quirky, Chicago-based software company that I profiled in *Bring Your Human to Work*, has a birthday celebration they can truly call their own.

It was back in 2007 when Harry Gottlieb, the founder of Jellyvision, along with Allard Laban, the chief creative officer at the time, decided it was time to turn the tables on their president, Amanda Lannert—who had been in charge of birthdays for years. Given Lannert's role, she never got called out for her own birthday. So Gottlieb and Laban suggested they celebrate Lannert's birthday.

In that first year, 17 employees gathered to celebrate Lannert's birthday. By the next year 30 or so Jellyvision employees decided they should go an extra mile and have all the guys grow out their mustaches. I told you they were quirky! All of the guys grew their facial hair, took pictures, and, voilà! A ritual was born.

Today, Jellyvision has more than 400 employees. Now, when they celebrate Lannert's birthday, aka Mustache Day, they are a big presence. The occasion has evolved into quite an elaborate ritual, with people dressing up in costumes. "Now, when we show up at Fogo de Chão, we take up the entire restaurant. And wearing and/or growing mustaches has evolved into dressing up in elaborate costumes, usually with a team theme. But the purpose of Mustache Day will never change: to celebrate our fearless leader Amanda's birthday . . . and to have a lovely, happy day with our colleagues, while eating an unholy amount of food."[9]

I love the way this basic birthday celebration started so organically and grew into an incredibly, only-at-Jellyvision ritual we can all aspire to.

Being seen is a human need, and we need our presence to be reflected back to us. We'd all be so much better off if we accepted this and folded it into our culture—at work, and everywhere else, too. It's not hard, but the simplest, even silly efforts go a very long way.

We're All in This Together: Rituals That Connect the Collective

So far, we've looked at rituals that celebrate people as individuals—their achievements, their milestones, their presence. Now we'll take a look at some amazing collective rituals that remind entire teams and companies, as we all learned in *High School Musical*—we're all in this together.

Celebrate Pride

If it's June at DoSomething, it's Pride party month. CEO Aria Finger told me, "We have a Pride party every June. Five years ago, our chief growth officer was gay, and he was like, 'Yo, we should throw a Pride party because 30 percent of our office identifies as LGBT,' and so now we have this tradition." Would people miss the Pride party if it went away? Heck, yes! This makes it a ritual in my book (and this *is* my book!).

Celebrate Joy

Sharyn Cannon, the chief culture officer at Tauck, a family-owned travel company that's landed on *Travel + Leisure's* "World's Best" list for 22 consecutive years,[10] told me about how one day she realized that so many of the employee communications were about recognizing a sad occasion, paying condolences. She wondered, "What about the good things? Why can't we celebrate those?" Thus, The Joyful Celebration was launched. During the month of November, a time when people are already thinking about gratitude, everyone at Tauck comes together to celebrate. What do they celebrate, you might ask? Anything joyful. This past November, Lynn Corcoran celebrated her 30-year wedding anniversary and the renewing of her vows on the Le Soleal cruise ship. Kiri Clark shared that her 17-year-old son, Fisher, officially started his journey to become a pilot. And Liz Malett celebrated her great team of colleagues in HR. Cannon went on to share, "[The Joyful Celebration] has lingering effects. A week from now I will hear, 'I didn't know that you just became a grandmother, that's great!' It just perpetuates for weeks and months even after. So sharing good news is very important, too. We try to do little things like that." Tauck's ritualized gift of joy keeps on giving.

Drop the Ball

In addition to her Attagirl ritual at the children's hospital, Shanna Hocking came up with a great way to infuse her fundraising staff with renewed excitement and motivation at the end of their fiscal year, June 30th. While that day marks the end of the year and the hard work associated with it, the excitement is often short-lived when employees realize that, when they come to work the next day, like in *Groundhog Day*, the clock resets and they start all over. It can be overwhelming. So Hocking had the idea to throw a "New Year's Eve" party on June 30th to pause and celebrate the (fiscal) year that's ending and generate excitement about the year to come. "We have black and gold streamers and confetti and even a ball drop." They also write New Year's resolutions and make toasts. What a way to repurpose a well-worn ritual.

Make Backroads Magic Together

Under the leadership of founder and CEO Tom Hale, for 40 years, employees at the adventure travel company Backroads have gathered together for a multiday trip. The idea behind the trip is that to truly understand the joy of active travel, staffers need to experience it for themselves.

Every year all 400 employees are invited to partake in an all-expense-paid four-day trip as a way of celebrating and seeing them. The trip consists of, "a veritable explosion of epic biking, hiking, laughing, bonding, eating, toasting, costumes, and dancing known as the Staff Ride!"[11]

Here is one staffer's report: "Six massive buses, filled to the brim with excited Backroads employees representing 20 different countries, departed rainy Florence and climbed the winding roads to Abbazia di Spineto, an eleventh-century stone abbey at the edge of Val d'Orcia, a UNESCO World Heritage Site. All around me, there were Trip Leaders being reunited, telling stories, singing, laughing, and joking with each other. I had the distinct sense, as I took in the cacophony, of being the new kid at summer camp. Luckily, by the time we arrived at our destination, I'd already had a chance to get to know quite a few of the super-friendly people around me."[12]

She continued, "Our bus pulled off the main road and followed the narrow cypress-lined path to the abbey. From the window, we could see row after row of bikes waiting. I don't think I really understood just how many of us were on the ride until I saw those 350 bikes!"

She describes the thrilling (or grueling, depending) leg-pumping trip up and down the hills of Tuscany—one big group, eating and drinking its way through the small towns, bonding, hiking, partying, resting. At the end, she reflects, "I began the long trip back to the Bay Area. The same person, but changed. It may seem like one big crazy fun party—and it is—but it's also more than that." How so? According to this particular Backroads employee, it's a ritual that is "true magic."[13]

 YIELD FOR RITUALS

Most companies have rewards and recognition programs, but they're often a bit on the rote side. They're definitely not magical. One of the litmus tests of a ritual is whether or not people would lose their minds if it went away. When searching for good opportunities for rituals, start where your company or team already has programs in place, and just up your game. Incentives, milestones, celebrations are all business as usual for most companies. Instead of trying to reinvent the wheel, try adding rituals to what you already have. And then keep an eye out for magic.

RITUALS ROCKSTAR

Bill Koenigsberg

The Man Behind the Curtain

Many of the leaders I've spoken to over the years have a trope or a mascot that serves as their inspiration. Bill Koenigsberg, CEO of Horizon Media, is no exception. His north star is actually the Wizard of Oz. He even has a mural of Dorothy and her friends on the Yellow Brick Road on their way to the Emerald City painted in the office. In fact, the Yellow Brick Road led him to create one magical ritual that truly makes his employees feel like a part of the company (as you may recall, the most fruitful question I've asked everyone I've interviewed for this book was: *When do employees feel most like employees*

(continued)

RITUALS ROCKSTAR *(continued)*

of your company?) When I asked this of Koenigsberg, he didn't hesitate. "People feel most like Horizon Media employees during our summer and winter celebrations. It's 3,000 people coming together."

The highlight of the summer party is the Wizard of Oz Award, which goes to someone who makes magic. As Koenigsberg described it, "The Wizard made magic. He was able to give the Tin Man this, the Scarecrow this, and send Dorothy home, so it is someone who makes magic here every day above and beyond anyone else." This person gets called up to receive the award and, "the place goes wild. . . . I would say that is one place where people really feel connected." Koenigsberg took me over to see the mural. Across from it are plaques dedicated to each winner.

An added bonus of the summer and winter celebrations is giving employees the chance to connect with Koenigsberg himself. "Everybody knows they can come see me at any time, but it's at these two parties that I will walk around, and everybody comes up and wants to talk to me and connect with me," he explains.

Being able to actually see someone at a party might not sound like much. But for employees at a big company with a rockstar CEO, it's a big deal, like seeing the man behind the curtain.

Koenigsberg uses rituals to take his company over the rainbow. That's what rockstars do.

CHAPTER EIGHT

"FIRST SIP"

Why Starbucks Is a
Rituals Rockstar

In the introduction to *Bring Your Human to Work*, I shared the story of meeting Ashley Peterson, the inimitable Starbucks barista who inspired my first book. I had gotten to know Ashley as part of my own personal daily ritual, which entails a visit to my Upper West Side Starbucks where Ashley always had my grande, extra-hot soy latte ready and waiting. Over the years, Ashley also grew to know my family, and all of our favorites. One day, Ashley sprinted out of the store to give my daughter Caroline a gingerbread cake she thought Caroline might like. Ashley's out-of-the-box gesture really touched me and changed the way I think about what it means to be human at work.

Today, a few years later, some things have changed while others have remained the same. I still visit Starbucks every day. I've added an extra shot to my coffee—maybe related to the fact that I now have three teenagers who stay up too late. Ashley has been promoted and promoted and now manages her own Starbucks. Her new shop is too far away for me to get to first thing in the morning, but I make a point to visit whenever I find myself in Midtown.

Last year, during a visit to Ashley's store, she filled me in on her new role as a store manager and asked me what I was working on. I told her I had just started working on my second book—about rituals at work. Ashley jumped into a story about how she leads all her new partners (the name for employees at Starbucks) through a coffee-tasting ritual on their first day of work. I thought, wow—*Ashley really is a woman after my heart*—thinking she created the ritual on her own.

But then she went on to share how *everyone* in the company, in every role and every location, has gone through the same ritual. As Ashley continued talking, she lit up, telling me how much this coffee tasting means to her and the people on her team and how it's a way to spark a shared passion for coffee in every single Starbucks partner. It even has a name—it's called the First Sip.

I had been on the lookout for a company for a deep-dive, a rituals exemplar to examine and discuss in one chapter near the end of the book. Walking out of the store, it dawned on me that, because coffee is such an important, ritualistic part of so many people's lives, the Starbucks internal rituals might be extra impactful. Maybe Starbucks was the rituals rockstar I had been looking for.

I was right.

Three P's, a Map, and a Guide

Starbucks has over 31,000 stores in nearly 80 countries, and their net revenue exceeded $26.5 billion for the fiscal year 2019.[1] Though I know Starbucks is always looking for ways to up their game, I think it's safe to say their performance is in good shape. And rituals, truly personal ones, as I discovered, are at the root of everything Starbucks does.

In *Onward: How Starbucks Fought for Its Life Without Losing Its Soul*, Howard Schultz, Starbucks' longtime chairman and CEO, now chairman emeritus, writes, "A well-built brand is the culmination of intangibles that do not directly flow to the revenue or profitability of a company, but contribute to its texture. . . . I always say that Starbucks is at its best when . . . creating enduring relationships and personal connections. . . . Starbucks is intensely personal. Aside from brushing their teeth, what else do people do habitually every day? They drink coffee. Same time. Same store. Same beverage."[2]

No wonder I feel like I belong at Starbucks! Every morning, rain or shine, I need my coffee. Trust me, you don't want to hang out with me if I haven't had my fix. When I travel, I choose hotels with a Starbucks in the lobby or nearby. It's not a big surprise that Starbucks' success relies on loyal customers like me whose personal rituals include their coffee. But it's another thing—and the point of this book—to consider how rituals can work within a company, transforming everyday routines into workplace magic.

I soon learned that the ritual Ashley introduced me to isn't just for onboarding new partners. Pretty much every day— at meetings, at events, at meals, and at celebrations, at every opportunity—their entire rituals roadmap is punctuated with a coffee tasting, not just in the product development and sales departments, but across the entire company. What better way to keep people feeling like they belong and connected to the purpose and mission of this coffee business? Coffee is at the center; it keeps everyone tied to the company's purpose, which is "to inspire and nurture the human spirit—one person, one cup and one neighborhood at a time," and the culture incorporates this very personal experience of coffee. As soon as I started diving into my research, I began to get a sense that Starbucks' coffee rituals would pass the Three P's test with flying colors.

Schultz claims, "the seed of what blossomed into today's Starbucks Coffee Company," came into being when he took a trip to Milan, a trip that changed the way he understood his job as the head of marketing for Starbucks' four stores in 1982. "Early one day . . . I popped into a small coffee bar. *'Buon giorno!'* an older, thin man behind the counter greeted me, as if I were a regular. Moving gracefully and with precision, he seemed to be doing a delicate dance as he ground coffee beans, steamed milk, pulled shots of espresso, made cappuccinos, and chatted with customers standing side by side at the coffee bar . . . I sensed that I was witnessing a daily ritual."[3]

It's this ritual that Schultz brought back with him to Seattle and has now shared with millions around the world. It's this ritual that—if taken away—would make people (like me) go crazy.

After reading everything I could about Starbucks, I reached out to people I could interview about coffee rituals. Everyone I talked to told me the same thing: the person I needed to connect with was Michelle Burns, the senior VP of global tea and coffee, someone who's been with Starbucks for over 20 years.

Finally, after much scheduling ado, the stars aligned, and I had my first chat with Burns. On the call, she told me about how even though Starbucks headquarters has multiple coffee shops inside the building (a dream come true!), she visits a different Starbucks store every morning on her way to work. One reason, of course, is to check in on the store and to stay connected to the brand and customers. But equally as important for Burns, her coffee symbolizes a personal transformation from home to work. In other words, she transforms from mom to executive. It's important for Burns to make the switch before she gets to the office.

Voilà! A magical transformation with coffee in hand.

Next, having hit it off with Burns and craving more, I went to Seattle for a visit.

That's when and where Burns told me, "You call it a ritual. We call it what we do."

And that's when I knew I'd found my guide through the rituals roadmap—one of the most successful companies in the world. In this chapter I'll take you through all the ways Starbucks uses the rituals I described in the previous chapters. Marking every stop along the way, they've created a truly exceptional rituals roadmap for success.

The Quintessential Starbucks Ritual: Coffee Tasting

I walked into Starbucks headquarters, and it didn't disappoint. It's like Disneyland for coffee lovers with a new (opened circa 2018), shiny, beautifully curated (with both swag and Italian pastries) cafe on the first floor. The space is beautiful. It is ultra-modern, with dark wood, tons of different cozy seating options, and two indoor campfire-type fireplaces. Burns suggested we sit in the corner in two large leather club chairs and that we start our chat over a shared, freshly brewed French press. I put almond milk in mine. I've had Starbucks coffee with almond milk, oh, at least a thousand times, but there's nothing like getting it straight from the source. It was sublime.

After chitchatting a bit about my travel, this book, and our kids, Burns talked me through a big-picture tour of the Starbucks rituals roadmap, tracking how coffee tasting is found throughout the employee experience, from an employee's first day of work until the last. Every step along the way on the Starbucks roadmap is a Three P's playground, ensuring partners feel psychological safety, belonging, and purpose at every turn.

It made perfect sense to kick off my coffee education and immersion with my very own coffee tasting with two esteemed members of Burns's Coffee Team: Andrew Linnemann and D. Major Cohen, known to all as Major. This kickoff did not disappoint. Their cup of coffee passion runneth over.

Linnemann kicked off our official coffee tasting, sharing coffees with me before the rest of the world got a glimpse. "The cup on your left is our brand-new Siren's Blend™. It's an homage to all the women pioneers in coffee. The coffee business is a male-dominated industry—if you look at tobacco, alcohol, they're just classic industries where it's just been the man-thing. [Then] in walked Mary Williams, Starbucks' second leader of coffee, and she changed everything. This blend is a nod to her and all the other trailblazing women in coffee." It didn't take long to feel the passion that this coffee team has, not only for the cup of coffee we were tasting, but also for every part of the sustainable supply chain that helped get it to our table.

Linnemann continued, "The second coffee is Sumatra in a French press. If you go back and forth between the two cups, you can start noticing differences." I did, indeed!

While sharing this classic Starbucks tasting ritual, Cohen couldn't contain his excitement:

> I'll tell you a great story about Sumatra. I had the joy of being [the leader on a bus] when we took partners to visit Sumatra. I had been talking about Sumatra for 23 years and had never been there. Many times the coffee comes from a family that has a home and a little yard, a garden, and they're growing coffee. Little by little those small amounts of coffee get collected until we get the quantities we need. What was described to me in the early days involved blue tarps next to people's homes, with 10 or 15 or 30 pounds of coffee on them. I wanted to validate that.
>
> The day that we were going to go out on the road, I found my seat on the bus, and I started taking

pictures out of the windows of the blue tarps next to people's homes. When I got to about 20, I realized that the story was totally true. Every house practically has a little bit of coffee, and at that time, they were drying it in their side yards. It was just amazing to me that—it hasn't changed.

I was drinking in every word as I sipped my coffee. Linnemann piped back in, "When you smell this coffee, you smell everything, you know. And then we taste it. We talk about how this is where you can be the child your mother didn't raise you to be, and we slurp it. . . . It's so cool because you get so much flavor profile. It's insane."

I couldn't argue! The coffee was rich, bold, and strong. In a word—insane. I thought back to Howard Schultz and his inspiration for the coffee-tasting ritual as a way of translating his passion for coffee to every single new partner . . . and then to every customer.

Mission accomplished.

After the tasting, my head was spinning, and it wasn't just from the caffeine.

The First Sip: Onboarding at Starbucks

If you ask any Starbucks barista what he had to drink at his First Sip, he might pause, smile, and immediately recount not only the drink, but also the perfectly paired accompaniment: "Ethiopia Harrar 1998, paired with chocolate-covered blueberries."

The First Sip is what Burns calls "the ritual foundation" upon which a career at Starbucks is built. As we learned in Chapter One, "All Aboard," the competitive race for talent is making it more important than ever that we bring people in and create community from the get-go. We have to start as we mean to go on. When people are hired as baristas, they begin by meeting someone like Ashley, their store manager, for their tasting and orientation.

The hands-on coffee experience isn't reserved just for the Starbucks customer-facing positions. The same thing unfolds for all of the nearly 5,000 employees in the Seattle headquarters, regardless of whether a partner is in sales or tech support or accounting. As Burns told me, "Your first day and moment with your manager almost always starts with coffee at the foundation."

While it's not so unusual for onboarding to begin the same way for all employees in an organization, it is pretty special to begin with something one can smell and taste, especially since our senses are so closely linked to how memories are made. "The richness is around the ability to share the experience together . . . and it usually [revolves] around stories," including asking people to recall the first time they tasted coffee or what a certain flavor reminds them of. These stories are yet another way to help make this a personal, even family experience, as Burns explains.

But, let's say, in contrast to Starbucks, you don't sell coffee. You sell experiences, widgets, services, whatnot. What, then, does this coffee ritual have to do with you? Well, it's not about coffee. As Burns reflected, "It's like the conduit to the conversation, with coffee as sort of the connector." The trick is to find something that connects employees with the feelings of the consumer. Then, work to keep it alive. Let's be honest—repetition is a key to rituals, but when we humans do things again and again, they can get a little dull. Starbucks, for example, makes sure to keep its rituals real by "de-program-izing," i.e., making sure they're authentic learning experiences because, as Burns said, "The intention is this is a part of a fabric or our fiber versus a check-off box."

All this emphasis on the First Sip is a lot, right? During a break in my conversation with Burns, I wanted to see what I could find online. It all sounded maybe just a wee bit exaggerated, even to a believer like me.

Well, shame on me. This is what I came across from a Starbucks Partners Facebook group (with 380,000+ followers).

The post asked: Do you remember what coffee you had at your first sip? Responses included:

- Pike Place Dark Roast no cream or sugar.
- Arabian Mocha Sanani, wild and exotic!!!
- 1 year ago on the 25th of Sep. I believe I tried either Sumatra or Cafe Verona, each tasteful on its own.
- Ethiopia, which ended up being my fave coffee and then they discontinued it.
- 20 years this month! I can't remember what my first tasting was, it's been too long! Lol. I remember going to a class called "Communicating Coffee" and had my mind blown by all I didn't know about coffee. In fact, when I applied to Starbucks I had never heard of it before! I just knew I wanted to work at a coffee shop! Thank you Candace Garcia LaMare for hiring me! 🖤
- I remember having a delicious cup of Lightnote Blend . . . 1998. 20 delicious and wonderful years ago.
- Guatemala. 7 years ago.
- 12 years on the 12th and it was Kenya paired with lemon loaf.
- 10 years ago this month. Pike Place Roast was just launched earlier that year. First tasting was with an oatmeal cookie. The rest is history.

The First Sip ritual is a Three P's home run. A sense of psychological safety and belonging is linked directly to purpose, history, and storytelling. Starbucks partners start as they're meant to go on: with sincere coffee passion. But beginning rituals at Starbucks don't stop at onboarding! Pretty much every day at Starbucks stores and at the headquarters, they start their day off with coffee as well.

Every morning at the Seattle headquarters, the company hosts the Nine at Nine ritual, so named because it happens on the ninth floor of the building at 9:00 a.m. It's a simple coffee tasting with a pastry pairing, and all are welcome. This is open to everyone who works there, not just the coffee people. Cohen and Linnemann from the coffee team shared with me, "What's really crazy about it is that at first it was hosted by the coffee team. But we opened it up to volunteers to lead the tasting, and we now have over 60 volunteers who work in different disciplines (from accounting to human resources) in the building who do the tasting once every 35 or 40 days."

March Through the Arch with a Cup in Your Hand: Beginnings and Endings

As I said in Chapter Two, opening rituals are best paired with closing rituals. Like the arches at Northwestern, bookending rituals make for extra magic. The Starbucks coffee tasting is no exception. As a rituals-rich company, Starbucks incorporates coffee when it's time to say farewell, too.

By chance, I have a friend from my business school days who was an executive at Starbucks but left before I was writing this chapter. I was able to ask both him and Burns about any rituals relating to his departure. He told me that Starbucks hosted a coffee tasting for him as a farewell and that it was so meaningful, there was "no bigger honor." As Burns affirmed, "It's community time. It's family time, right? There's something—there is a celebratory nature to it."

Imagine being held together like that in a parting of ways. That's one of the gifts of the Three P's. Parting ways is often an awkward, if not contentious, experience. Employing rituals can help ease a rocky transition, reminding both parties to celebrate everyone's success and to stay connected. Parting can be sweet sorrow, sure, but it's also an opportunity for new beginnings.

Meetings

In Chapter Three, I talked about how rituals in meetings can help create purpose, presence, and a way to chime in and chime out. I was delighted to learn that in "every meeting here at Starbucks—we always want to start a meeting with a coffee tasting. This is just a welcoming way to kind of break the ice and have a moment before you get into whatever your meeting topic might be." The experience of drinking coffee brings people, literally, to their senses, and helps them be present. The ritual tasting is also the perfect way to chime in (and, perhaps, cleaning up after the coffee might work well as a chime-out). Burns added, "Something we always really try to promote is comparing two coffees at the same time because when you taste something by itself . . . you have no basis on which to compare," an action that ties everyone right back to Starbucks' purpose.

So again—we have a Three P's extravaganza. Burns then shared the team's commitment to the ritual with me, "Even this morning, we had a team leadership meeting [and someone said] 'Hey, can somebody please bring some coffee?' I don't think I saw anybody reply, so we all made sure to bring something. We all sat down, like nine of us, and we had a tea and two different coffees. And we went through all of them. You can't have a meeting without coffee—you just don't show up empty-handed."

This ritual isn't just a way to spruce up everyday status-report meetings. During my chat with Burns and Cohen, Cohen told me, "When we have a meeting in our town hall or open-forum environment, the coffee's the ritual and the story's usually bigger and broader and connected to it, you know what I mean? It just happens all day, every day."

Yes, I definitely know what he means.

Eatings

At Starbucks, coffee tastings are often paired with food as a way to enhance the experience. A biscotti, a pastry, a piece of chocolate—a bite and a sip complement each other perfectly. At Starbucks, eating is not as ritualized as drinking, but it's not to be forgotten. Like wine with meals, pairing a coffee with a cake makes them both better.

Professional Development

Starbucks Coffee Academy is an online collection of courses available to Starbucks partners who want to level up on their coffee knowledge with 100-, 200-, and 300-level courses. But they're not just limited to Starbucks partners. Courses are an open-source opportunity for anyone who wants to learn about the basics of roasting and blending, brewing, and sourcing. The best part? They're free!

When Burns and Cohen told me about this, I first thought the academy sounded like a brilliant way to invite everyone to take professional development about coffee quite personally, but I wondered if, like many big corporate programs, this was a bit more marketing than magic.

That's what I thought until Burns told me that thousands of people signed up for the academy when it initially launched in September, 2019. And the number continues to grow. That's a lot of very professional development!

"One of the things that many of us in coffee education do when we open up a class anywhere in the world, . . . We always ask them, 'What's your coffee ritual?' We bring people along the journey," Burns told me. "[The journey] goes all the way through the supply chain and the specifics that are part of the makeup of our entire company."

Whether a dedicated Starbucks employee or simply a coffee enthusiast, the Starbucks Academy allows for and celebrates one's learning and growth.

But how does this high-level thinking come down to partners? Through rituals, of course. Simply by beginning each class with a "What is your coffee ritual?" as an icebreaker, Starbucks adds a personal touch into each professional development course and invites people to bring their own rituals in. This is a great way to weave rituals into professional development, especially if you don't know where to begin when designing rituals. When you ask people to share their own rituals, you not only spark inspiration for rituals you can incorporate into your company culture, you are also showing your people that you care, opening the door for new opportunities to learn and grow.

Another deeply impactful professional development ritual involves an actual physical journey—it's called an Origin Trip. Burns explained, "We take small groups of coffee leaders from within the company to an Origin experience to be able to get a very deep understanding of our coffee and the farmers and communities that grow it. The focus on the community becomes the much bigger picture of understanding the role coffee plays in these communities. We have a deep responsibility to make a postive impact in the lives of farmers and their families and most importantly to ensure the future of coffee for all."

Partners from around the world travel to Sumatra, Costa Rica, and Rwanda. They learn about how coffee travels from "the first 10 feet"—the coffee farms—to the "last 10 feet," where people like you and me around the world enjoy their morning ritual.

According to Starbucks' multimedia journalist Joshua Trujillo, during these trips, "the partners will visit farms, tour farmer support centers where farmers learn about sustainability, help plant coffee trees, and discover how the beans are processed. They will see drying tables where the coffee is dried and raked by hand by the coffee producers, and meet the people working in the fields. It's also a chance to experience the pride and passion many people in Rwanda share about the strides they have made in recent decades."[4]

A rituals trip like this goes well beyond the professional and clearly touches people personally. When a group moves through a big experience like international travel, it's a rite of passage that binds them together. Rituals that people share make it so they will always have shared stories and experiences to refer to—together.

The Coffee Break

Inspired by the Italian coffee bar, Starbucks *is* the coffee break for 100 million weekly visitors[5] taking a break from work around the world. This includes people who are taking a very big break from their workplace and are making Starbucks their home office away from home.

In Italy people stand up and sip their espresso, then leave their cup on the counter before they begin their day. In the United States, we sit down, sometimes for a long time, or we walk with our paper cups, bringing our coffee break with us (multitaskers that we are!). In China, people traditionally prefer tea as their beverage of choice, which of course Starbucks sells in China. But somehow Starbucks is managing to spread their coffee gospel even in that market. In fact, Starbucks is opening an average of one store in China every 15 hours![6] People in China also like to gather for coffee in the afternoons instead of mornings like we do, but that just gives Starbucks an opportunity to create new rituals.

As we know, and as I mentioned in Chapter Six, the smoke break—thank goodness—is a thing of the past, at least in the United States. I'd love to see a coffee takeover! Imagine a ritual where teams get up and break for coffee like at Slack (remember when I nearly jumped out of my skin with the gong?) with the same passion as they used to do for nicotine. A ritualized coffee might be just the inspiration people need to step away from their desks.

We See You: Rituals for Recognizing and Rewarding

In Chapter Seven I talked about how important it is for employees to feel rewarded for their efforts at work and to feel seen for being who they are. Contrary to popular opinion, this desire is not true just for millennial or Gen Z workers. Not even close. All human beings share the need to be recognized.

I highlighted three kinds of rituals that help companies do this—rituals that reward for performance, rituals that celebrate people for just being there, and rituals that connect the collective.

Here's a story from Burns and Cohen that combines all three rituals into one. When they shared this with me, I got goosebumps.

In 2019, 12,000 store managers gathered in Chicago for the company's Leadership Experience. Cohen was responsible for ensuring McCormick Place—173 conference and breakout rooms and three ballrooms—had coffee.[7] How much coffee, you ask? Well, not counting breakfast (a mere 800 to 1,000 gallons), that's 4,582 gallons to be brewed per day. If Starbucks partners can't show up to a casual meeting "empty-handed" they certainly can't go without at such a big event!

Cohen recalled, "The team and I actually got up at 1:30 a.m. and went to McCormick Place to start brewing the thousand gallons . . ."

If I wasn't impressed already by the Herculean task of brewing on this level, Cohen continued by telling me the best story of all:

"There were 400 volunteers in the back of McCormick Place who couldn't go to the United Center for one of the larger sessions. So, we had a viewing party. I came in [early] and brewed 24 gallons of the same coffee, and right when our leaders were onstage [doing the tasting with the whole big group], I wheeled in a 24-gallon shuttle of coffee so the volunteers could experience it as well."

I wanted to clarify: "You made coffee for the 400 volunteers, so they could have their coffee tasting with the rest of the company?"

In other words, Cohen went to all that trouble so that the volunteers' efforts could be recognized? So that nobody had to feel like they were just the invisible coffee brewers behind the companywide celebration? So that everyone on the entire team—including those who couldn't attend—felt psychologically safe, like they had a purpose, and were performing at their best because of it?

And he said, "I mean, it was really cool."

Very cool, yes. But now I know: It's just what they do.

YIELD FOR RITUALS

Starbucks is a giant on the global stage with a product that is one of the world's favorite rituals. But even the Mom and Pops among us can emulate what they do— they keep it simple by returning to coffee at every step along the employee roadmap. What is your company's coffee? What do you sell or make or offer that you can ritualize and transform into magic?

RITUALS ROCKS

Ashley Peterson

Ashley Peterson is one helluva human.
Starbucks is a rituals rockstar of a company, and of
course Ashley Peterson, the Starbucks barista who
inspired my first book, is the ultimate, individual rockstar.
Not only is she one helluva human being, a mom and
kind heart, she's an incredible brand ambassador who
doesn't just talk the talk. She talks it to everyone who
walks through the door.

   I recently visited Ashley at her new Midtown store.
We hugged like we always do, and then Ashley actually
lifted me up off the ground! A regular customer—whom

(continued)

RITUALS ROCKSTAR *(continued)*

Ashley knew, of course—observed, "Wow! You two are really excited to see each other."

(Have I mentioned that I love this woman?)

Ashley and I sat down at a table in her store, drank coffee (Ashley was excited to make me my "usual"), and then we talked about rituals. Like all great leaders, Ashley gives credit where credit is due: "My prior store manager, Aubrey Hensley, taught me, when you're having a conversation, never start a conversation without coffee. That is now a part of the culture that I brought to my team, as a store manager. [Coffee is present] whenever I have a meeting or a conversation with them."

As a store manager, Ashley attended the recent gathering in Chicago. I was so excited to get her insider's take on it. This is what she said:

> Everybody got the coffee at the same time; it was still hot. I was so inspired because we heard stories about some managers and how they are as people and how they want to show up at work. Most of the time, you never know what somebody is going through, and you never know how you are making somebody's day. For CEOs, most of the time, you feel like they just want results, numbers, and sales, but for Starbucks now, they want to focus more on the customer experience. . . . It has always been a part of our culture, and now they are digging deeper.

She told me that each store manager was empowered to develop a purpose statement for their store. Ashley and her supervisors picked: "To make people happy through their experience at our store." As Ashley put it,

"Everything we do should lead back to that purpose. No matter what our customers have gone through in their lives, I want them to leave here happy." Based on my experience, it's working!

Making New Yorkers happy is a tall—actually a "venti"—order. But if anyone can do it, Ashley can.

Of course, being the quintessential human leader that she is, Ashley created a ritual in her store that connects her team members to that purpose. Each morning, she does a "check-in" with her staff. She makes sure they're dressed properly, she reviews the store goals for the day, and then she revisits the store's purpose and asks each partner to make a commitment for the day: " 'You'll be behind the bar. What are the commitments that you'll be making today? For instance, making eye contact and saying good morning.' She moves from person to person. Each role has a set commitment."

That's at the beginning.

Then, at the end of the shift, she provides feedback to the partners on how they performed against the commitments they made in the morning. She single-handedly encourages engagement through rituals.

That's marching through the arch, and then doing it again.

Ashley transforms everyday routines into workplace magic.

CHAPTER NINE

TIDYING UP

Rituals at the End of the Roadmap

In 2018, I published my first book on how to make the workplace more human by honoring relationships. Then, I traveled around the world talking to companies about how they could bring their human to work—through, for instance, values, meetings, disconnecting to reconnect, and professional development. I started to see something really interesting: sometimes the smallest actions led to the biggest wins. Again and again, I saw that the companies or teams that seemed most engaged and productive came together in a variety of micro-ways: they engaged in traditions, parties, awards, retreats, and gatherings that seemed magical. While it makes sense that people will want to throw big money at big problems, sometimes the simplest, most human solutions work best.

That's when it occurred to me that all these little ways I was seeing had something in common—they all seemed like rituals, as they're dear to the people performing them, and they're powerful beyond their practicality. The more I learned, the more I recognized that rituals are actually *the tools of the human workplace*. And they don't have to cost a thing. With these insights in mind, I set out on a tour of companies that use rituals to create a human workplace. After traveling around the country and speaking with so many different leaders and rituals rockstars, I've taken what I've learned and designed a roadmap to help individuals and leaders transform everyday routines into workplace magic. This is what I've learned about rituals at work.

As we have seen in Chapters One through Eight, rituals help us feel less anxious and more safe, connected, and purposeful. Even before the stress of COVID-19, we've been hungry for a healthy dose of all that! Just consider rituals rockstar Marie Kondo and her incredibly successful, often life-changing magic of tidying up. She understands that the simplest actions can have a huge effect. Before tossing an old bra, plate, or drawer of rubber bands out on its ear because it does not "spark joy," Kondo invites people to verbally thank the household item for its efforts. This particular ritual might not resonate with everyone (*GQ* writer Nicole Silverberg wrote of this eccentric goodbye, "I mean . . . I love you, girl, but no"[1]), but what

I think is valuable isn't what's uttered to the joyless item, but rather the fact that there's a ritual to help people say goodbye. The tidying guru's rituals are so effective at getting people to let go of whatever doesn't spark joy that thrift stores across the country can hardly keep up.[2] Rituals get the job done.

All's Well That Ends Well

Rituals inspired me to begin this journey, and they can help us all tidy up at the end, too—at the end of a project, a day, a week, or a book. I'll share some of my favorites.

Do You Miss Me?

Perhaps you recall my favorite ritual-mining question: *When do you and people on your team feel most like yourselves?* Perhaps you also remember my most reliable ritual testing question, the best way to discover if something is truly a ritual: *Would you miss it when it's gone?*

The folks at GoHealth Urgent Care, a state-of-the-art urgent care center business, currently operate in nine states across the country. In addition to the incredible work they do every day, I love them for the way they have ritualized the simple question, "How was your day?" to the point that the question is a core part of their culture. They couldn't live without it. They would absolutely miss it if it were gone. That's how we know it's a ritual.

This is no ordinary healthcare center. For starters, on their website, they say, "WARNING: Our Centers May Induce Smiles."[3] I must confess, when I visited a center in downtown Manhattan, I left smiling. I wasn't there for a health problem, true, but I never would've imagined an urgent care center with so much thought put into it. From the reception desk, to the rooms, to the colors used—everything was designed to create a sense of psychological safety for the patients, a clear sense of why the staff went to work every day—their purpose—and a healthy, successful, and healing performance for all.

Gary Weatherford, the chief customer officer (CCO), was clearly very passionate about his work, and, after our conversation, I could understand why. He told me stories about the staff at GoHealth going above and beyond to help their patients. He mentioned their "EOD" practice—a simple email that one person, typically the medical assistant or the radiology technician, sends out at the end of the day to fellow workers about events of the day. Recipients of the EOD include the CEO, COO, CCO, and CHRO, signaling that leadership wants to know about issues, big and small, that have impacted a particular location. Around one in three EODs receives a direct response from the local leaders. The EOD can be just a few lines or a full-blown story, such as the humorous one where a routine illness led to a surprise, positive pregnancy test. The couple was "so overwhelmed with joy that they both began crying hysterically." Weatherford told me, "It's healthcare, so there are moments that are very emotional."

Not only did this strike me as a wonderful way to keep abreast of what's happening in the 145 (and counting) centers across the country, but, as Weatherford reflected, "It is a very powerful way of staying connected." He meant the staff would stay well connected to the leadership team, but this simple practice also keeps staff connected to themselves and to their patients.

This EOD ritual is one part management tool and one part process that uplifts human engagement. Weatherford continued, "This is something that we ask [people] to do. And I don't think they realize that the CEO's going to read that and reference it." But the entire GoHealth leadership team does, in fact, read every EOD, and, Weatherford acknowledges, "They kind of bring a tear to your eye."

We don't have to get teary to have a purposeful experience that helps us feel like we belong. But it can't hurt.

This simple, streamlined process that asks so little of people delivers so much for GoHealth. It delivers 145 daily, in-the-trenches reports to the executive team. They eagerly read up to all 145 reports every evening or early next morning, but no one's complaining. Weatherford insists that the staff at GoHealth, "wouldn't think of leaving the center (or ending their day) without pressing send on their EOD."

This is a perfect example of a ritual that's imprinted into people—in this case both the senders and receivers of the EOD. And if it disappeared (recall the snack cart from the Introduction?), something would feel very wrong.

At first, this may seem like nothing more than a standard procedure with no frills about it. After all, there is nothing special about a standard end of the day report to your superiors. But what makes this standard practice ritualized is the human element that it brings. Real rituals are enmeshed in the very fabric of a culture and so very human. GoHealth is a modern medical facility, and sharing stories about interactions with patients is exactly that. It's a reminder of what ties us all together— our humanity. I love this ritual because of the way it falls into that sweet spot between "tech" and "connect." There's nothing fancy about it; it's data-rich but not data-driven. It doesn't cost a dime. It's just a good old-fashioned question, celebrated at closing time: "How was your day?"

TGIF

Happy hour on Friday is a tried-and-true ritual for a reason. Going out for a drink with your work colleagues and friends is a great way to unwind, connect, and cap off the week. But it's not the only way, nor is it always the most inclusive way. End-of-week rituals are a perfect opportunity to advance the Three P's, so it's a good idea to make them accessible to everyone, including people who have to get home to kids, elderly parents, or pets, not to mention introverts, nondrinkers, or people who may feel like they don't immediately "fit" with the group that's going out together.

Here are examples of some clever and inclusive Friday rituals that require neither a drink in hand nor a babysitter:

- At Glamsquad, Friday afternoons are for pampering. Glamsquad cofounder David Goldweitz explained to me, "We have a lot of engineers who suddenly decide that they

really like pedicures having never had one in their lives."
So on Friday afternoons everybody gets to indulge.

- Abby Falik is the CEO of Global Citizen Year, a company
that facilitates an amazing global gap-year program for
students who want to take a year off between high school
and college. Falik told me that every Friday, someone hits
the gong for their afternoon "Deck," a group workout
of sit-ups, push-ups, and pull-ups using a deck of cards.
How does it work? Decide what kind of exercise you and
your team want to do, flip over a card, and do that number of sit-ups, push-ups, etc. (jack = 11; queen = 12; king
= 13; ace = 1). "It takes about 10 minutes start to finish
and everyone leaves feeling pumped!"

- At Knotch, a data-driven media company, every Friday is
show-and-tell time, which goes well with Knotch's value
of transparency. At 4:30 p.m., people get together to chat,
and given that it's the end of the week, the timing just
feels right. To create a little more direction than just "let's
hang out," someone came up with the idea of sharing
weird dreams and celebrity sightings in addition to show-
and-tell. I asked Garrison Gibbs, head of HR, to walk
me through a recent show-and-tell. "Our head of sales
shared a new iterative of a product demo, an employee
who had just taken a trip to Africa shared photos, and we
celebrated two new hires. And I'm always on the lookout
for celebs." Some recent sightings included Gigi Hadid,
Kylie Jenner, Paris Hilton, and Gibbs's favorite, the cast
of Law & Order because it was being filmed right near
the office.

- At Chipotle, just after 10 p.m., the doors are closed, and
though the customer service portion of the day comes to
an end, many of the rituals are just beginning. Store manager Patrick Vasquez told me that at his store, some of his
coworkers have formed a barbershop quartet, "just singing all night," which is particularly sweet, since at this
Chipotle, "the ultimate goal is that nobody goes home
until everybody is done." What a way to create a feeling

of safety and purpose. A team that sings and cleans together definitely crushes it together.

The P.S. Ritual

The final close-out rituals I'm going to share in this chapter are not for closing out a week or a day, but rather for closing out an event or activity. I call it the P.S. ritual.

Remember the Haka dance from Chapter One, the ferocious show of intimidation the All Blacks perform at the beginning of their matches? I never would've thought that story could get any better. But then I read an article about a lesser-known All Blacks ritual called "Sweeping the Shed." "Sweep the Shed" is the All Blacks' code for saying, "Clean out your lockers." After every game, this simple activity is elevated to the point of ritual in order to keep these hulking players humble. As Peter Abela points out in his *Medium* article, "Though it might seem strange for a team of global superstars to act in this way (especially when it is someone else's job to carry out this task), humility is core to their culture. The All Blacks believe that it's impossible to achieve stratospheric success without having their feet planted firmly on the ground."[4] How cool is it that they have "a tradition that says that no individual is bigger than the team and its ancestors. Everyone is responsible for the smallest details—including cleaning out the locker room after training or a match."[5] For the All Blacks, their humility—a core value—is rooted and reinforced in ritual.

Finally, at JetBlue (one of my favorite companies that I talked a lot about in my first book), every single crew member aboard a flight (including the pilots), whether "working" officially or not, helps clean the plane. Even the CEO when he is onboard a flight puts on those blue gloves and digs into the seat pockets. Why? Because it's a ritual. Everyone does it. Cleaning together creates a feeling of belonging and purpose, which is good for performance, especially since it connects to every single one of JetBlue's core values: safety, caring, integrity, passion, and fun.

This JetBlue ritual is so ingrained that a friend of mine who used to work at JetBlue tried to help out the crew after a flight. But his offer to lend a hand was politely declined. While he understood, he admitted that he just didn't feel quite right.

He felt like something was missing.

Marie Kondo's latest book is called *Joy at Work*, which I'm eager to read. Her book tour, like everything else these days, has been cancelled. When asked about how she was handling this moment, she responded, "It is a challenging and uncertain time, but it may also be an opportunity to express gratitude for your space and to tidy up if you've been wanting to."[6]

Kondo turns to the ritual of tidying up to transform her everyday routines into workplace magic.

What will you do?

CHAPTER TEN

DESIGN YOUR OWN ROADMAP

Congratulations! You've made it to the end of the roadmap. You've learned about rituals from a wide variety of companies and leaders, and hopefully you're feeling inspired. Thank you for allowing me to be your trusted guide.

ROADMAP SPREAD

So, you might ask, what now? How can *you* use rituals as the tools to create a human workplace?

1. **Start by creating your own unique map.** Discover the rituals that your organization—however big or small—already has in place across the employee lifecycle, paying close attention to the following:

   - **Recruiting and onboarding:** You only get one chance to make a first impression. Recruiting, interviewing, and hiring are all prime rituals real estate, inviting new hires (and candidates) into the fold. Chances are, your company already has a set of processes for all of these things. So think about how you can add a little TLC to them. Perhaps every candidate is greeted with a smile and a cup of coffee, tea, or hot chocolate. Maybe every new hire receives a welcome pack with candy and snacks. Whatever you choose to do, make sure it fits with your company brand and sets the tone for how you want potential and new candidates to view your company from the very first impression.
   - **Beginnings:** Start as you mean to go on. Rituals are a natural way to begin the day or the week (or really anything) with intention. Beginnings provide employees time to pause, reflect, and connect. You can easily take something you already do in the morning with your employees and make it a beginning of the week ritual. Remember that a ritual is 100 percent intentional. So even something as simple as sending a morning

check-in email with intention at the beginning of each
week can be made into a ritual. Best-case scenario: sur-
round your experience in magic by opening *and* closing
with ritual.

- **Meetings:** Given the number of meetings employees
  attend every day, this is one of the biggest opportunities for rituals. For meetings in the human workplace,
  more than assembly is required. Begin each meeting
  with a moment for employees to ground themselves or
  find their center. Start off with a round robin show-and-
  tell with everyone in the room. The important thing
  to remember for meetings is to make everyone feel like
  they can contribute if they want to. Think about how
  many meetings you've attended where you felt like your
  ideas weren't heard. However you choose to ritualize
  your meetings, do it in a way that makes everyone feel
  included and heard.

- **Eatings:** Channel your inner firefighter, and transform
  your meals into rituals. Remember, it doesn't matter
  what you eat or where you eat it. The most important
  meal of the day is the one we share.

- **Professional development:** The best professional development is personal. What better way to say, "We
  appreciate you" than to give employees the opportunity to grow themselves professionally and personally?
  Consider the example of LinkedIn, and inspire your
  employees with rituals that help them grow on the
  job—up, down, and sideways. That's what people want;
  it's the human way to learn. Making a ritual out of
  professional development is the next logical step to making your employees feel connected. You don't have to
  dedicate a whole day to it like LinkedIn does, but think
  about what your company already does for professional
  development and add in the personal touch necessary to
  make it a ritual.

- **Taking breaks:** Rituals that help us pulse our attention
  make us more productive. Whether it's a one-minute

dance party, a few push-ups, or a walk around the block to get some air, regular breaks are good for the health of your people and your business.

- **Recognition and milestones:** It's only human to want to feel seen and to feel recognized. Whether it's once a year or every week, rituals are an important tool in the human workplace to reward performance, celebrate milestones, and connect individuals to the collective.

2. **Perform a rituals litmus test to see—are they, in fact, rituals? Are the Three P's at work?**

- Do they provide Psychological safety?
- Are they linked to Purpose?

If the first two are a yes, then you can be sure that your ritual is Performance-enhancing.

- Finally, would people Protest if it went away?

The easiest way to test this is to put yourself in your employees' shoes. So, let's say you've decided to incorporate the snack cart from the Introduction into your company rituals. If you were an employee, and the cart stopped coming without warning one day, would you wonder what happened? Would it throw your whole day off? If yes, then you've got yourself a ritual! You can also test a potential ritual in real time. Introduce the ritual and then take it away after a few weeks and take note of everyone's reaction. Are people talking in hushed tones about what could have happened? Have you received any direct questions about what happened? Or is there no reaction at all? If people react negatively or wonder why the snack cart stopped coming, you've got yourself a ritual that's here to stay!

3. **If you don't have rituals, then what? Look for opportunities for rituals through the employee lifecycle in these ways:**

- If you want to create rituals, start with your company values. It's the best way to make rituals feel authentic and organic within your company.
- Remember that rituals can be top-down or bottom-up, so ask your team for ideas.
- Be willing to scrap rituals that aren't working, feel inauthentic, or feel like a box check.

Rituals are the tools of the human workplace—the place where we can bring our whole selves and manifest our values in a meaningful, productive way.

The world of work is always changing. But human beings' needs remain the same. After food, water, and shelter, we need each other. Rituals, as we've seen throughout this book, are just the thread to sew us close. Dr. Vivek Murthy, the surgeon general under President Obama, put it like this:

> The answer to how companies can address loneliness isn't pulling people together for a daily happy hour or the annual company party or picnic. We have to help people connect more deeply with themselves and give them opportunities to connect with others in deeper, more substantial ways. We all have a desire to be seen, to know we matter and to feel loved. That's part of being human.[1]

In other words, this rituals business is not just a feel-good exercise. When we're engaged at work—through rituals, through connection, through psychological safety and purpose—we become like the firefighters, outperforming those who let go of the rituals and traditions that keep us connected and feeling like we belong. Higher engagement leads to less stress, which leads to more creativity and resilience. Turnover goes down. Passion is turned up.

Whether you're facing a team, a global company, a day in your life, or an incredibly awkward task, like doing karaoke in front of strangers, rituals can turn your everyday routines into magic.

Once you experience the power of rituals for yourself and your company, you won't stop believing.

RITUALS IN TURBULENT TIMES

On March 16, 2020, everything changed for me. My fellow New Yorkers and I went into lockdown. The world of work in the United States transformed overnight as entire states were instructed to stay home. Offices, restaurants, stores, and schools closed. Approximately 30 million people were receiving unemployment benefits as of May 2020, reflecting a 16 to 19 percent nationwide unemployment rate.[1] The economy nearly shut down, and the stock market actually closed. We'd never seen a threat this big or this real.

At the same time, as frightening as it's been, I've never been so inspired.

Overnight, home offices sprang up. Parents became home-school teachers. Americans galvanized to send masks to frontline workers and donations to the millions that were out of work. We began reaching out to one another for support, more raw and vulnerable than at any time in recent history.

It soon became clear that regardless of age, gender, or circumstance, many of us began turning to rituals to help us during these scary times. From the mass rituals like the 7 p.m. New York cheering of the frontline healthcare workers, to company Zoom parties, to family game nights, to individual mindfulness practices, the repetition of our lives in lockdown inspired many of us to discover the power of rituals.

Dr. Heidi Grant, a social psychologist out of Columbia, says that "rituals make us value things more."[2] That's the magic. Rituals make everyday, ordinary things special. But how? As we've seen again and again throughout our ride around the rituals roadmap, rituals work when they're authentic—when they truly matter to us. As Grant puts it, "*Personal involvement* is the real driver of these effects."[3]

When we take our rituals personally, they help us feel more connected to others. That's the magic.

As we've seen in the preceding pages, rituals provide us with what every human needs—psychological safety, belonging, and purpose. This has never been more apparent. Since COVID, I've heard from many people who are discovering for themselves what science has been telling us all along—rituals are restorative and give us a sense of control when everything else feels out of control. Research shows that rituals help us deal with grief, and it doesn't matter if the rituals are super-serious, age-old, and passed down from generation to generation or made up on the spot and utterly ridiculous. *Harvard Business Review* senior editor Scott Berinato writes that rituals "give people a sense of control and familiarity in a new and uncomfortable situation."[4]

Uncomfortable, indeed.

To be honest, it's hard to believe that as I complete this manuscript, my speaking career has screeched to a halt. I'm working from home with my three teenagers and husband, and we're entering a new phase of the pandemic throughout the spring and into the summer of 2020. My personal rituals are helping me through it all. I'm still getting my Starbucks every morning from the drive-through, taking my 8:00 a.m. Pilates class with my teacher and good friend Karen (virtually), and having Taco Tuesday with my family.

But that's just me. Or is it?

Before closing this new chapter of the new normal, and the final chapter of this book, I decided to take a ride of my own around the rituals roadmap to see how rituals work under these challenging conditions of uncertainty and stress and with most people working remotely. I reached out to some of the folks I highlighted in the book and asked them for updates on how their rituals were faring under quarantine. Can rituals *still* turn everyday routines into workplace magic?

Spoiler alert: the answer is *yes*! While some stops on the roadmap are easier to translate to a virtual experience than others, rituals are just the magic we need in this very turbulent time.

Recruiting and Onboarding

In the May 2020 issue of the *Harvard Business Review*, Mary Driscoll and Michael D. Watkins wrote an article called "Onboarding a New Leader—Remotely." Count virtual onboarding among the many things we never would have imagined!

While their article focuses on leaders, the principles work for any and all employees: "First, be crystal clear about expectations. . . . Since they won't be learning informally from those around them, schedule briefings on critical issues related to their role. Assign them a virtual onboarding buddy . . . and consider bringing in a coach."[5] Sounds easy enough! Set expectations, stay connected, and offer lots and lots of support.

But how can we weave rituals in?

I asked Aria Finger, CEO of DoSomething, a holder of many rituals (more on her stuffed penguin ritual later) about how their first remote onboarding went. This is what she said.

"We keep sharing our weekly 'tissue issue' which highlights new employees if someone started the previous week." (It is called the tissue issue because it's a publication that is usually taped inside the bathroom stall for employees to read.) "We also still do 'coffee buddies,' introducing them on Slack to the team and sending an email around on the first day to get to know them and congratulate them. We also still do 30/60/90-day check-ins with them to make sure they're feeling good."

And then: "It went . . . okay. Not gonna lie, not as well as it would have in the office!"

Being authentic and transparent like Finger is exactly what every company needs. Under any circumstances.

Beginnings

Remember Avner Mendelson, CEO of Bank Leumi USA, who does a ritual check-in at the beginning of every day with his senior team? His team shares a quick round of updates, something they are each stuck on, and it ends with someone sharing a values story—my favorite part. I reached out to ask him if he and his team continued this ritual during quarantine, and the answer was a resounding *yes!* (Though he sometimes moves the ritual to the end of the day—hey, during a crisis, you've got to be flexible!)

Here's an example of a story about the values Care and Passion that came up during the pandemic.

> The only people that go to the office go two or three times a week to pick up the mail and send it to people in that department at their homes. This one guy, Ray Diaz, who sent the mail, saw there were a couple of really important client documents that were supposed to arrive and didn't arrive, and they weren't getting responses from FedEx. [So] he drove to FedEx at a Queens distribution center to look for them and was able to find them by physically going there. Again, this is an example of the care and passion of going above and beyond for people and clients. It is just amazing. This guy—you know, the mailroom guy — who goes above and beyond because he cares. It is just incredible.

A ritual that brings rockstars like Ray Diaz to light is a ritual worth fighting for.

Another example of a ritual worth fighting for is the walk through the arch at Northwestern, which is the iconic beginning of every Northwestern student's education and is also bookended by students at graduation. I saw an Instagram post about a fellow whose sister was so disappointed that she couldn't march through the arch that he built her her very own arch to walk through! He writes: *My sister didn't get to walk through the @northwesternu arch when she graduated because of Covid, so I built a 21ft replica in my parents driveway! Congrats Beth, can't wait to see what the future holds for you.*

I love the lengths to which people will go to maintain their rituals—especially during the times that matter most.

Meetings

Have you ever heard of a mullet meeting? I heard this term during a virtual talk I gave recently, and it cracked me up. It's a meeting that's business up front, party in the back. And this is how many meetings are run these days, over Zoom, like *The Brady Bunch* meets *The Office*—a wacky combination of work and play.

Remember the Udemy Meeting Hero Pledge and the cute little mascot hanging up in their meeting rooms? Well, those rooms are empty now. But Cara Allamano, SVP, people, places and learning, told me they just launched "Meeting Super-hero," which is their meeting hero for this work from home time. It takes a superhero to help us manage our meeting mania these days.

I asked her how they managed to keep their meeting culture alive as they peer into each other's living rooms, closets, kitchens, and lives. Udemy added a Friday morning coffee chat with the CEO called Kitchen Table talks. As Allamano told me, "We see it as an extension of how we share meals together [in the cafeteria] and how important the table is to us." Meetings and eatings often go together—some rituals are made for each other.

Since this is no time for formalities, Allamano told me that Udemy's CEO Gregg Coccari joins some meetings with "his dog at the table." And they added some technology that allows people to ask questions, which gives the meetings "a little more of the feeling that you would actually get live and in person."

When I asked Allamano how she thinks this new working from home reality has affected her workforce, she said something I hadn't considered: "One of the things that I think has happened since we have this global workforce is it has made everybody more empathetic to the people who frankly have been [working from home] this whole time. I think we are getting to be way better communicators because of it, just because we are realizing, 'Oh, when you are in that boat, you don't always know everything just through osmosis and just being around people.' I think it [will make us] much better at integrating those other offices into the day in and day out."

I'm sure Udemy's superhero will help them find the perfect rituals for doing just that.

Eatings

Udemy's Lunch Roulette—a beloved ritual I described earlier in the book—randomly assigns four or more people to share a lunch. Lucky for Udemy's employees, Lunch Roulette is still bringing together people who crave connection over virtual lunch. Once the leaders at Udemy saw how many people were requesting a spin of the wheel, they decided to actually pay for people's shared virtual meals. It's that good for business. I was so excited to hear this was still happening, I wanted to share the good news with companies who might want to do the same kind of thing, so I asked Allamano for more details.

Just like pre-COVID, people can opt in for Lunch Roulette, then they receive an email telling them who their lunch partners are. In the past this was done by office because people were having lunch in person, but Udemy has opened this up and has been doing more coffee/snack chats across time zones to ensure connection between offices.

In addition to supporting local restaurants with takeout orders, Allamano sees how good it is for folks to connect, even over Zoom, and the plan is to keep it going like this for some time because, sadly, as she put it, "we are in a marathon, not a sprint."

While the pandemic has made it impossible for me to join Chipotle for another one of their pre-shift meals, the crew has continued their ritual of eating together before opening their stores for delivery and curbside pickup. When I learned of this, I reached out to Marissa Andrada, chief diversity, inclusion and people officer at Chipotle, to learn more.

I soon learned that, just like the rest of us, "the challenge we've had is also ensuring that we have social distancing . . . so unfortunately the ability to eat close together has been more like . . . they are still eating at the same time, but they have to eat at least six feet apart." Like for so many of us, this important ritual remains the same, but instead of a family-style dinner around the table, it's "more like sitting around the dining room."

Trust me, after months of dining with nobody but my husband and kids, I'll take it!

Professional Development

It wasn't long before I began my work from home life, adjusting as well as I could to everything virtual all the time, that I started to wonder about how I was going to start upskilling on my own. I had come to rely so heavily on all my travel and networking and IRL connecting to keep learning and growing. Which made me wonder about LinkedIn's InDay. Once a month, the company gathers together around a theme as a way of investing in their culture and their employees. Before COVID, as I describe in the book, I had the pleasure of visiting the NYC LinkedIn offices on InDay for their Day of Wellness. I meditated, I danced, I ate from their gourmet cafeteria. I felt great!

So, I wondered, how is InDay working virtually?

Very well, it turns out!

Nawal Fakhoury, LinkedIn's leader of employee experience, who showed me around InDay in person, has been busy hosting virtual InDays during COVID. The first theme during this time was "Family." For all of us in lockdown with our kids, how perfect is that?

While InDay is an opportunity for LinkedIn employees to honor the given theme in any way they see fit, scheduled programming is available for those who want to take advantage. One popular opportunity for Family InDay was the "Bring a

Loved One Call" people shared with their teams. Fakhoury invited her mom to teach public speaking skills, "a total proud-daughter moment." Another team member hosted a virtual cooking session, with her adorable seven-year-old daughter who cooked "exotic pasta salad."

Another team member wrote, "Today was Family InDay at LinkedIn. Once a month, the company encourages employees to invest in themselves and their communities. And today, more than any other InDay, was a day I fully invested. . . . I spent the day with my newly expanded family. Nearly two weeks ago, we welcomed our son . . . into the world. Both my husband . . . and I are blessed to have generous parental leave policies, which have allowed us the space and time to focus on becoming the family unit we want to be. The time away from work to bond with Aiden and with ourselves has been invaluable, and I don't take that for granted."

While not a parent herself, Fakhoury spent part of her Family InDay connecting with a team member's kids over Zoom. "We spent our time painting, talking TikTok, and learning what you'd spend your money on if you won the lottery."

Of course, folks chimed in on their InDay threads saying they wanted Fakhoury to be their kids' babysitter!

I see a ritual in the making.

As Fakhoury wrote on her LinkedIn page, "There's something so adorable and heartwarming about your professional and personal world colliding."

That's what I call taking professional development personally.

Since Udemy is a learning platform with an amazing professional development ritual called DEAL (Drop Everything and Learn), I had to ask how they were faring during lockdown. I asked Shannon Hughes, VP of communications, for an update. When I asked her if they still do their 3:00 p.m. Wednesday one-hour ritual of learning whatever the heck people want to learn, she said, "Yup. [And quarantine] has made it more special, I think, because people are looking for ways to be connected."

When I asked her how things have changed, she said, "There has been even more sharing around what people are learning. . . . It is just fascinating to look at it through the lens of ritual and see the strength and the importance of those things that have flowed through, from something that informally started to something that now we are formalizing. We are asking our managers to go through the work from home canvas, think about all the elements that are important to people's work and lives, and figure out how we make that real for them."

I'm so glad I asked.

Taking a Break

Working from home conjures up images of people in PJs, moseying over to their computers when they feel like it. Oh, how COVID has killed that fantasy! For those lucky enough to have a job, it's been grueling to keep up with the business at hand, while homeschooling older kids and trying to entertain and occupy younger ones, all in the midst of trying to stay healthy. Before quarantine, we were a nation addicted to work, but now we're just in over our heads. And we need a break more than ever.

I decided to check in with Tim Brown, the cofounder of Allbirds, the cool shoe company where employees drop for 40 push-ups every day at 4 p.m. At least, they used to.

I was thrilled to discover that Allbirds employees still do their ritual push-ups, but with a hilarious work-from-home twist. Each day, an employee volunteers to videotape and share the 40 at 4, and I count myself among the fortunate few who— outside of Allbirds employees—was able to actually see one! The video I saw was produced by April (her silly screen name is *Aprol*) and her cat, Luna.

"Welcome to 40 at 4," April says to the camera. "Today we are going to be doing 40 at 4 with friends. And by friends, I mean small domesticated animals because we are in self-isolation. Let's go." April then does 40 pushups with her furry cat on her back. She carried the cat up and down the stairs 10 times, followed by shoulders and abs. I loved the disclaimer at the end: no animals were hurt during the production.

Not surprisingly, videos like this inspire a lot of engagement on the Slack channel.

Sixty people had something to say about April's video. I know I'd look forward to a treat like that every day. We think this is a moment in time we'll never forget, but in no time so much of this will be a blur. I think we'll be happy to forget a lot of it, but for moments we'd like to cherish, rituals can work their magic.

Reward and Recognize

As you may recall, DoSomething's stuffed penguin is passed from person to person as a gift of recognition, a simple way of saying, "We see you, and you're awesome." I was delighted to hear that the award is still happening during COVID. Finger shared with me how it was recently awarded to a relatively new employee and the impact that it had. While the penguin itself is quarantining in DoSomething's Manhattan office, the impact of the recognition continues.

Every Wednesday, the staff member who received the penguin the week before gives it to someone new. It's always a surprise. After the new employee received it, she sent a message to Finger that said, "This is going to get me through the pandemic. This is so meaningful and so kind, and I have all of those wonderful thoughts from my coworkers which is going to get me through."

In addition to the boost of recognition, the penguin holder gets an added bonus—the winner gets to pick the music theme for the Friday weekly "Power Hour." Each week the playlist is announced via Slack, and people can just directly add to it and make comments like, "Ah, what a jam, thanks for adding Waterfalls." According to Finger, "Playlist examples are far-ranging, everything from 'songs of summer' to 'songs by Black artists' to 'one-hit wonders from your middle-school days.'"

Another awesome ritual!

So, what did the new employee do to win the bragging rights of the penguin? According to Finger, "She stepped up by switching teams. She was hired onto the business development team, and we have less work right now. The marketing team said—we need you on talent, on relationships and new partner outreach. And she said, 'Awesome.' Now she is splitting her time because it's what the organization needs."

It sure sounds like that penguin is in the right place.

If I didn't love Chipotle before the pandemic, I'd be a fan now. Wow. When I reached out to Marissa Andrada, chief diversity, inclusion and people officer, for an update on the ritual meal, she also sent along a video that brought me to tears. Every year, as a ritual, Chipotle gives out the Adobo Awards—so-named because adobo is one of the main ingredients in Chipotle's chicken—recognizing and rewarding high-performance players in the company. This year, the awards were handed out over video which began with an image of Las Vegas and these words:

The Adobo Awards are Chipotle's highest honor. A chance to honor the best-of-the-best at our Manager's conference in Las Vegas.

Then they cut to all these images of huge crowds, lights, and teary award recipients on a stage, then these words: *This year, we knew the show had to go on.*

That's when we see Brian Niccol, CEO, in a tux, on his computer screen, announcing the virtual award ceremony. Behind the scenes, the award recipients were told they were getting on a pretty standard Zoom call to be interviewed for a promotional video. But instead, they were greeted by Niccol or Andrada or Scott Boatright, chief restaurant officer, and told, "Congratulations! You won this Adobo Award!" And over video we watch people in their Chipotle uniforms receive their awards with smiles, tears, and gratitude for their teams.

The looks on these people's faces were truly magical.

In April, *Forbes* predicted that Chipotle would be one of those businesses to come out of the pandemic "stronger than ever."[6] I asked Andrada why Chipotle seemed to be able to make the COVID switch so seamlessly in their business as well as in their rituals.

As you may have guessed, it's all about the values.

"Every decision that we have made is based on our values. I think that is really the thread of our culture. I look at other organizations which are scrambling and how they are making decisions, when for us it is about what we're doing to cultivate a better world and what we're doing to live our values. I think people see it. . . . You already know that, but I think that is the center of all of it."

Tidying Up

Aimée Woodall, the founder and CEO of Black Sheep, is our rituals rockstar from Chapter Six on taking a break. I checked in with her to see how she was faring during this crazy time, and she shared how she and her Black Sheep are maintaining one of their 10-year-old rituals that keeps them feeling connected to each other.

She wrote me right back.

"What STRANGE times we're living in. I was thinking about you this week as we spent our first week working from home, all 18 of us, and decidedly adapting our rituals for this new way of life. We had #ChampagneFriday virtually today."

Champagne Friday has been a tradition for the creative agency as a way to celebrate their accomplishments from the week. In the past, they combined Champagne Friday with what they call "Tiny Victories."

Woodall explained that before COVID, "Tiny Victories are celebrated every day in our office (we have a "register" or journal that we log them in that hangs under a "Tiny Victories" neon sign—oh, I miss that sign—where we write them down as they occur), and while we collect them along the way, this Friday tradition helps us to pause, celebrate each other, connect, and recognize the things we have accomplished, both tiny and big, that lead to the bigger shifts for our clients and our agency."

Because Black Sheep is a fast-moving company where the work is rarely complete, "it's hard to remember to stop and celebrate the milestones and the hard things we have overcome, but it's so critically necessary for the long haul. . . . Now, in the middle of this crisis, we're doing that virtually. Every Friday, in front of our screens with a glass of wine, cocktail, sparkling water—whatever it may be. I don't think screen time will ever be the same as in-person gathering around the kitchen table in our office, but for now, it'll do. It has to."

For Black Sheep, ending the week with Champagne Friday, even if it's with a glass of water—like all rituals—really takes the edge off.

IDEO, another world-class design firm, discovered a new ritual during the pandemic. When the regular Monday lunch meeting went virtual, rows and rows of Zoom squares lined up on everybody's screen, and then, as a spontaneous sign-off that soon became ritualized, every participant waved into their camera then disappeared. As David Schonthal, an IDEO senior portfolio director, writes, "It was such a hit, the goodbye ritual is now performed and recorded every week, then distributed as a reminder of our shared time together until the next weekly meeting."[7]

Finally, I checked in with Andy Biga, SVP of people from GoHealth, to see how he was holding up as a leader on the front lines. This is the company that asks their healthcare workers to end each shift with a ritualized End of Day (EOD) report. I wondered what those EODs looked like these days.

Biga generously shared some of the most recent EODs.

April EOD

How was your day? Today Center X was busy, with one team navigating the drive through Covid-19 testing and the other seeing patients in the clinic. There were three positive Covid-19 results. Two legacy employees . . . came to help with the testing, a sincere thank you to them for all of their help. Together we were all learning to get a good flow. To end the day, we had an elderly walk-in patient at 7:55 p.m. We were sure to treat her like the first patient of the day, not the last! She was very grateful for the care and compassion. I cannot tell you how wonderful it is to work with such a great crew!

April EOD early in the NY Launch of Virtual Visits

How was your day? A great day for the virtual team. R suggested we assign each VCC with a provider, and that made the process of "triaging" patients much easier. It also allowed for our WhatsApp to not be going off the hook! This team worked well together and we all pitched in to provide patients with excellent care. Big thanks to A for helping out this morning with calls and transfers to sites, she really lifted a load off of us. The virtual world is getting busier every time I log on, and it's amazing to see how much this team is helping the community. A great way to end the week with the virtual team.

April EOD from a Physician's Assistant in NY

How was your day? As provider I want to say thank you to all the members in our leadership. Because of constant information updates, Q and A meeting, the most important thing is we don't need to worry about PPE supplies like other providers in the hospital where I work. I want to say thank you especially to K who always personally delivers supplies to CenterX when we are short . . . our operations director S who personally delivered one box of duck shaped N95 masks to me in R because the blue ones don't work on my face. Thank you guys and I am very confident that we will go through this tough time safely with leadership's full support.

April EOD from NY

How was your day? It was a busy day but we kept our heads above water. Walk-ins made it more challenging almost two hours over our closing time haha!!

April EOD from CT

How was your day? Today was another crazy phone call day, patients that came were seen for various reasons to keep them away from the ER and on a positive note, one of our first Covid patients that was seen back in March came in to thank us (all that saw her were here today). Not only did she write a beautiful note calling us her "heroes," she gave each of us a 100 dollar gift card to a local restaurant. That surely made our day and feel appreciated!!!

April EOD, from NC

How was your day? Today you could be standing next to someone who is trying their best not to fall apart. So whatever you do today, do it with kindness in your heart.

April EOD from NC

How was your day? Nothing should go back to normal. Normal wasn't working. If we go back to the way things were, we will have lost the lesson. May we rise up and do better. Reflecting a lot today on all the brave Americans battling this virus. Our hearts go out to family and friends facing all the unknown.

I'm with the GoHealth employee who says, "If we go back to the way things were, we will have lost the lesson." By all means, I can't wait to return to pre-COVID life. Believe me—I'm eager to go back to my office, get on a plane, as well as get a manicure, hug my friends, and sit in a restaurant. But it's also true that these turbulent times have taught us a lot, and I hope we remember it.

✦ ◆ ✦

David Gelles, an executive producer at CNN, writes power-fully about his own journey during COVID, quarantined in his parents' house with his small children after his mother died. He writes, "I've found that having a few daily rituals helps to make the pain a bit more manageable. In my family, one ritual involves two scoops of ice cream each night. The five of us—my dad, my wife, my kids and I—all gather at the kitchen table, while I take orders scooping out bowls to them."[8]

During these turbulent times, some companies have main-tained their current rituals. Others have created new ones. Rituals don't have to be big or complicated or fancy. They can come from the top down or the bottom up. An end-of-the-day email, a story about an employee living the company values, a funny video, or even a bowl of ice cream will do.

Because rituals are good for people, great for the business of being human, and will help all of us through good and tur-bulent times.

ACKNOWLEDGMENTS

This book was born out of a ritual. My daily stop at Starbucks for my grande, extra-hot soy latte led to meeting my favorite barista of all time, Ashley Peterson, which inspired my first book, *Bring Your Human to Work*.

And then, after *BYHTW* was published in 2018, I didn't have another book on my mind. But during a monthly dinner with a friend that had become a ritual, all that changed. Over a plate of pasta and with a glass of red wine in hand, it hit me that rituals are the tools of the human workplace. Book-writing is like childbirth: you forget about the hard parts and then you do it again. I wasn't really ready, but I held my breath and jumped in.

I could not have jumped in without my team that continues to support all that I do.

To Bethany Saltman who has been there every step of the way as a book partner, brand strategist, and collaborator. Thank you for urging me to go for it and being there to help me get it done. To Alexa Clements, *you rock*. You continue to add more insight and value with every new project, and you do it with precision and with a smile.

Thank you to my agent, Jane Dystel, who took a chance on me and continues to support my work. My editor at McGraw Hill, Amy Li, loved the rituals idea and quickly made it happen. Thank you to the rest of the McGraw Hill team (Nora Hennick, Amanda Muller, Peter McCurdy, Maureen Harper, and Daina Penikas) for your support in marketing, production, and getting this book out to the world.

Thank you to Paul Howalt for designing the cover and all of the fun, very human, spot-on illustrations in the book—and for the many, many back and forths. Thank you to Eric Gordon for his wise and generous continued work on my branding.

To my readers Amy Yenkin and Jodi Kovitz—thank you for putting in the hours to read these pages and provide the valuable feedback that made me a stronger writer. You'll see the fruit of your labor in the pages of the book.

To my husband, Jeff. Thank you for all that you do to support my work, including a close and careful read of both books, and for telling the world about my work. And thank you for changing your email signature to: *Proud Husband of Erica, Author of BYHTW. Order now (link included), and make me look good!* Everything that you do helps me look good and makes me want to do better.

Finally, to my children—Julia, Caroline, and Daniel. And Cruiser. I treasure my special rituals with each of you and our many family rituals—Taco Tuesday, Family Feud with bowls of Ben & Jerrys, family Pilates, and hikes. And especially the games of Hearts, Qwirkle, and Rummikub, which multiplied during the pandemic. I hope that these rituals bring you as much joy as they do me.

And, finally, this book is dedicated to my mother, Gail Rutkin, who passed away in April 2020. Given COVID-19 restrictions, I was not able to say a proper goodbye. She adopted two girls, my sisters Kiki and Crystal, when I was in high school. While my sister Lauren and I were decades older, different religions, and different races, it was my mother's devotion to creating our eclectic Rutkin family rituals (for instance a Christmas tree with blue and white decorations) that connected us, made us feel like we all belonged, and made all the puzzle pieces fit together.

Through rituals, my mother created a family.

NOTES

INTRODUCTION

1. Kniffin, Kevin M., Brian Wansink, Carol M. Devine, and Jeffery Sobal. "Eating Together at the Firehouse: How Workplace Commensality Relates to the Performance of Firefighters." *Human Performance* 28, no. 4 (2015): 281–306. https://doi.org/10.1080/08959285.2015.1021049.

2. Brooks, Alison Wood, Julianna Schroeder, Jane Risen, Francesca Gino, Adam D. Galinsky, Michael I. Norton, and Maurice Schweitzer. "Don't Stop Believing: Rituals Improve Performance by Decreasing Anxiety." *Organizational Behavior and Human Decision Processes* 137 (November 2016): 71–85. https://www.hbs.edu/faculty/Publication%20Files/Rituals%20OBHDP_5cbc5848-ef4d-4192-a320-68d30169763c.pdf.

3. Frame, Selby. "Julianne Holt-Lunstad Probes Loneliness, Social Connections." American Psychological Association, October 18, 2017. https://www.apa.org/members/content/holt-lunstad-loneliness-social-connections.

4. Popova, Maria. "The Difference Between Routine and Ritual: How to Master the Balancing Act of Controlling Chaos and Finding Magic in the Mundane." Brain Pickings, June 6, 2016. https://www.brainpickings.org/2015/02/13/routine-ritual-anne-lamott-stitches/.

5. Brooks, et al. "Don't Stop Believing."

6. Brooks, Alison Wood. "Research: Performing a Ritual Before a Stressful Task Improves Performance." *Harvard Business Review*, November 26, 2019. https://hbr.org/2017/01/research-performing-a-ritual-before-a-stressful-task-improves-performance.

7. Brooks, et al. "Don't Stop Believing."

8. Brooks, et al. "Don't Stop Believing."

9. Brooks, et al. "Don't Stop Believing."

10. Harter, Jim. "4 Factors Driving Record-High Employee Engagement in U.S." Gallup, February 28, 2020. https://www.gallup.com/workplace/284180/factors-driving-record-high-employee-engagement.aspx.

11. Watson-Jones, Rachel E., and Cristine H. Legare. "The Social Functions of Group Rituals." *Current Directions in Psychological Science* 25, no. 1 (February 26, 2016): 42–46. https://doi.org/10.1177/0963721415618486.

12. Watson-Jones and Legare. "The Social Functions of Group Rituals."
13. Hobson, Nicholas M., Juliana Schroeder, Jane L. Risen, Dimitris Xygalatas, and Michael Inzlicht. "The Psychology of Rituals: An Integrative Review and Process-Based Framework." *Personality and Social Psychology Review* 22, no. 3 (November 13, 2017): 260–84. https://doi.org/10.1177/1088868317734944.
14. Hobson, et al. "The Psychology of Rituals."
15. Seppälä, Emma, and Kim Cameron. "Proof That Positive Work Cultures Are More Productive." *Harvard Business Review*, May 8, 2017. https://hbr.org/2015/12/proof-that-positive-work-cultures-are-more-productive.
16. Seppälä and Cameron, "Positive Work Cultures."
17. Seppälä and Cameron, "Positive Work Cultures."
18. Gallup, "Item 10: I Have a Best Friend at Work." February 28, 2020. https://www.gallup.com/workplace/237530/item-best-friend-work.aspx.
19. Heffernan, Margaret. "The Secret Ingredient That Makes Some Teams Better Than Others." TED, December 7, 2015. https://ideas.ted.com/the-secret-ingredient-that-makes-some-teams-better-than-others/.
20. Hering, Beth Braccio. "Remote Work Statistics for 2020: Shifting Norms and Expectations." FlexJobs Job Search Tips and Blog. FlexJobs, February 13, 2020. https://www.flexjobs.com/blog/post/remote-work-statistics/.
21. Conger, Kate. "Facebook Starts Planning for Permanent Remote Workers." *New York Times*, May 21, 2020. https://www.nytimes.com/2020/05/21/technology/facebook-remote-work-coronavirus.html.
22. Edmondson, Amy C. *The Fearless Organization: Creating Psychological Safety in the Workplace for Learning, Innovation, and Growth*, xvi. Hoboken, NJ: John Wiley & Sons, Inc., 2019.
23. Edmondson, Amy C. *The Fearless Organization*, 42.
24. Keswin, Erica. Interview with Daisy Auger-Dominguez. Personal, March 9, 2020.
25. Travis, Dnika J, and Jennifer Thorpe-Moscon. "Day-to-Day Experiences of Emotional Tax Among Women and Men of Color in the Workplace." Catalyst, 2018. https://www.catalyst.org/wp-content/uploads/2019/02/emotionaltax.pdf.
26. Travis and Thorpe-Moscon, "Emotional Tax."
27. Lorenzo, Rocío, Nicole Voigt, Miki Tsusaka, Matt Krentz, and Katie Abouzahr. "How Diverse Leadership Teams Boost Innovation." Boston Consulting Group, January 23, 2018. https://www.bcg.com/en-us/publications/2018/how-diverse-leadership-teams-boost-innovation.aspx.
28. Hunt, Vivian, Sundiatu Dixon-Fyle, Sara Prince, and Lareina Yee. "Delivering Through Diversity." McKinsey & Company. Our Insights, January 2018. https://www.mckinsey.com/business-functions/organization/our-insights/delivering-through-diversity.

29. Robison, Jennifer. "The Future of Your Workplace Depends on Your Purpose." Gallup, February 28, 2020. https://www.gallup.com/workplace/257744/future-workplace-depends-purpose.aspx.

30. Fink, Larry. "Larry Fink's Letter to CEOs: Profit & Purpose." BlackRock, 2019. https://www.blackrock.com/americas-offshore/2019-larry-fink-ceo-letter.

31. Grant, Heidi. "New Research: Rituals Make Us Value Things More." *Harvard Business Review*, June 16, 2015. https://hbr.org/2013/12/new-research-rituals-make-us-value-things-more.

32. Vaccaro, Adam. "How a Sense of Purpose Boosts Engagement." *Inc.*, April 18, 2014. https://www.inc.com/adam-vaccaro/purpose-employee-engagement.html.

33. Rozovsky, Julia. "The Five Keys to a Successful Google Team." Google re:Work, November 17, 2015. https://rework.withgoogle.com/blog/five-keys-to-a-successful-google-team/.

34. Guenzi, Paolo. "How Ritual Delivers Performance." *Harvard Business Review*, August 7, 2014. https://hbr.org/2013/02/how-ritual-delivers-performanc.

35. Mesagno, Christopher, Daryl Marchant, and Tony Morris. "A Pre-Performance Routine to Alleviate Choking in 'Choking-Susceptible' Athletes." *The Sport Psychologist* 22, no. 4 (2008): 439–57. https://doi.org/10.1123/tsp.22.4.439.

36. Hobson, Nicholas M., Devin Bonk, and Michael Inzlicht. "Rituals Decrease the Neural Response to Performance Failure." *PeerJ* 5 (May 30, 2017). https://doi.org/10.7717/peerj.3363.

37. Moran, Gwen. "How to Harness the Power of Rituals to Improve Your Work." Fast Company, August 3, 2015. https://www.fastcompany.com/3049175/how-to-harness-the-power-of-rituals-to-improve-your-work.

38. Carr, Austin. "Three Rules for Creating Workplace Rituals to Improve Company Culture." Fast Company, November 15, 2017. https://www.fastcompany.com/40486190/three-rules-for-creating-workplace-rituals-to-improve-company-culture.

CHAPTER ONE

1. Cox, Jeff. "There Are Still 1.4 Million More Jobs Than Unemployed People, but the Gap Is Closing." CNBC, August 7, 2019. https://www.cnbc.com/2019/08/06/there-are-still-1point4-million-more-jobs-than-unemployed-people-but-the-gap-is-closing.html.

2. Selko, Adrienne. "4 Ways to Win the Talent War." *IndustryWeek*, October 10, 2018. https://www.industryweek.com/talent/article/22026488/4-ways-to-win-the-talent-war.

3. Bayly, Lucy. "New Weekly Figures Show Almost 40 Million People Lost Their Job Since the Pandemic." NBCNews.com, May 21, 2020. https://www.nbcnews.com/business/economy/new-weekly-figures-show-almost-40-million-people-lost-their-n1211886.

4. Deloitte. "Deloitte Global Millennial Survey 2019." Deloitte, May 24, 2019. https://www2.deloitte.com/global/en/pages/about-deloitte/articles/millennialsurvey.html#info.

5. McFeely, Shane, and Ben Wigert. "This Fixable Problem Costs U.S. Businesses $1 Trillion." Gallup, February 28, 2020. https://www.gallup.com/workplace/247391/fixable-problem-costs-businesses-trillion.aspx.

6. Gallo, Carmine. "A New Study Finds Most Employees Want to Quit, but There's a Simple Way to Keep Them Happy." *Forbes*, October 25, 2017. https://www.forbes.com/sites/carminegallo/2017/10/25/a-new-study-finds-most-employees-want-to-quit-but-theres-a-simple-way-to-keep-them-happy/#471e8a647d23.

7. Pew Research Center. "In U.S., Decline of Christianity Continues at Rapid Pace." Pew Research Center's Religion & Public Life Project. Pew Research Center, December 31, 2019. https://www.pewforum.org/2019/10/17/in-u-s-decline-of-christianity-continues-at-rapid-pace/.

8. Rugby World Cup. "New Zealand." Rugby World Cup 2019. https://www.rugbyworldcup.com/teams/new-zealand.

9. Guenzi, Paolo. "How Ritual Delivers Performance." *Harvard Business Review*, August 7, 2014. https://hbr.org/2013/02/how-ritual-delivers-performanc.

10. Daisley, Bruce. *The Joy of Work: 30 Ways to Fix Your Work Culture and Fall in Love with Your Job Again*, 65. London: Random House Business Books, 2019.

11. Cable, Daniel. "Starting a New Job Is Stressful. But What If There Was a Better Way to Do It?" TED, September 11, 2018. https://ideas.ted.com/starting-a-new-job-is-stressful-but-what-if-there-was-a-better-way-to-do-it/.

12. McFeely et al. "Fixable Problem."

13. Cable, "Starting a New Job."

14. Strack, Rainer, Jean-Michel Caye, Carsten von der Linden, Horacio Quiros, and Pieter Haen. *From Capability to Profitability: Realizing the Value of People Management*. Boston Consulting Group, July 2012. https://image-src.bcg.com/Images/BCG_From_Capability_to_Profitability_Jul_2012_tcm9-103684.pdf.

15. "Hiring and Firing: Evaluating for the Right Cultural Fit." Zappos Insights. Accessed March 5, 2020. https://www.zapposinsights.com/membership/hiring/lesson-1.

16. Varner, Kurt. "Why I'm Joining Dropbox." Medium, July 29, 2018. https://medium.com/@kurtvarner/why-im-joining-dropbox-b30f44ce3c61.

17. West Duffy, Mollie. "Beautifully Designed Employee Welcome and Onboarding Kits." Mollie West Duffy, September 10, 2016. https://molliewestduffy.com/designing-culture/2016/9/9/beautifully-designed-welcome-kits.

18. Daisley, *Joy of Work*, 166.

19. Fosslien, Liz, and Mollie West Duffy. *No Hard Feelings: The Secret Power of Embracing Emotions at Work*. New York: Portfolio/Penguin, 2019.

20. Henry, Zoë. "Why Kind Founder Daniel Lubetzky Invested $20 Million to Connect Kids Around the World." *Inc.*, October 17, 2017. https://www.inc.com/zoe-henry/kind-founder-empatico.html.

21. Lucas, Amelia. "Chipotle Staged a Comeback. Here's How It Plans to Keep the Growth Going." CNBC, November 5, 2019. https://www.cnbc.com/2019/11/05/chipotle-staged-a-comeback -heres-how-it-will-keep-the-growth-going.html.

CHAPTER TWO

1. Moran, Gwen. "How to Harness the Power of Rituals to Improve Your Work." *Fast Company*, August 3, 2015. https://www .fastcompany.com/3049175/how-to-harness-the-power-of-rituals -to-improve-your-work.
2. Amador, Cecilia. "Coworking Is the New Normal, and These Stats Prove It." AllWork, May 10, 2019. https://allwork.space/2019/05 /coworking-is-the-new-normal-and-these-stats-prove-itt/.
3. Owl Labs and Global Workplace Analytics. "State of Remote Work 2019." 2019. https://www.owllabs.com/state-of-remote -work/2019.
4. O'Connor, Clare. "Undercover Billionaire: Sara Blakely Joins the Rich List Thanks to Spanx." *Forbes*, April 12, 2016. https://www .forbes.com/sites/clareoconnor/2012/03/07/undercover-billionaire -sara-blakely-joins-the-rich-list-thanks-to-spanx/#5acbc8b0d736.
5. Hoffman, Reid. "How to Find Your Big Idea: Sara Blakely, Founder of Spanx." *Masters of Scale*, March 20, 2018. https:// mastersofscale.com/sara-blakely-how-to-find-your-big-idea/.
6. O'Connor, Clare. "Inside Forbes' Historic $10 Billion Richest Self-Made Women Cover." *Forbes*, July 12, 2016. https://www.forbes .com/sites/clareoconnor/2016/06/01/inside-forbes-historic-10 -billion-richest-women-cover/#114afc0c5f84.
7. Keswin, Erica. Interview with Jodi Kovitz. Personal, January 6, 2020.
8. Rozovsky, Julia. "The Five Keys to a Successful Google Team." Re:Work, November 17, 2015. https://rework.withgoogle.com /blog/five-keys-to-a-successful-google-team/.
9. "DEI in Action: A Radically Human Approach to Case Studies." Promise54. Accessed March 7, 2020. https://casestudies .promise54.org/.
10. Daisley, Bruce. *The Joy of Work: 30 Ways to Fix Your Work Culture and Fall in Love with Your Job Again*, 28. London: Random House Business Books, 2019.
11. Newport, Cal. "The Rise of the Monk Mode Morning." Study Hacks Blog. Cal Newport, February 24, 2017. https://www .calnewport.com/blog/2017/02/24/the-rise-of-the-monk-mode -morning/.
12. DesMarais, Christina. "Here's How the Highest Achievers Start Their Days Differently Than Everyone Else." *Inc.*, January 15, 2018. https://www.inc.com/christina-desmarais/14-morning-rituals -successful-executives-swear-by.html.
13. Zipkin, Nina. "How Spending 60 Minutes Doing This Every Morning Helps This Entrepreneur Prepare for the Day." *Entrepreneur*, February 23, 2017. https://www.entrepreneur.com /article/289626.

14. Azevedo, Mary Ann. "Meditation App Headspace Closes on $93M Series C, Eyes Continued Global Expansion." Crunchbase News, February 12, 2020. https://news.crunchbase.com/news/meditation-app-headspace-closes-on-93m-series-c-eyes-continued-global-expansion/.
15. DesMarais, "Highest Achievers Start Their Days."
16. "The Heart of the Designer Community." Dribbble. Accessed March 7, 2020. https://dribbble.com/about.
17. "We Design Experiences That Make You Feel Welcome." Dflash. Accessed March 7, 2020. https://www.dflashcultureboards.com/.
18. Leopold, Wendy. "Weber Arch Dedicated." Northwestern University News, June 8, 2011. https://www.northwestern.edu/newscenter/stories/2011/06/weber-arch-dedication.html.
19. Agrawal, Radha. *Belong: Find Your People, Create Your Community, and Live a More Connected Life*, 3. New York: Workman Publishing, 2018.
20. Agrawal, 7.
21. Daybreaker. Accessed March 24, 2020. https://www.daybreaker.com/.
22. Agrawal, 145.
23. Agrawal, 145–46.

CHAPTER THREE
1. Koehn, Nancy. "Half of All Meetings Are Unproductive. Is There a Fix?" Marketplace. Minnesota Public Radio, April 27, 2019. https://www.marketplace.org/2013/09/24/half-all-meetings-are-unproductive-there-fix/.
2. Atlassian. "You Waste a Lot of Time at Work." Atlassian. Accessed March 8, 2020. https://www.atlassian.com/time-wasting-at-work-infographic.
3. Doodle. "The State of Meetings 2019." Doodle Blog, 2019. https://en.blog.doodle.com/state-of-meetings-2019-2/.
4. Morrison, Jim. "The Cost of Rising Seas: More Than $400 Billion (and Lots of Angst)." *Wired*, August 21, 2019. https://www.wired.com/story/the-cost-of-rising-seas-more-than-dollar400-billion-and-lots-of-angst/.
5. Parker, Priya. *The Art of Gathering: How We Meet and Why It Matters*, ix. New York, NY: Riverhead Books, 2018.
6. Zak, Paul J. "The Neuroscience of Trust." *Harvard Business Review*, November 27, 2019. https://hbr.org/2017/01/the-neuroscience-of-trust.
7. Zak, Paul J. "How Oxytocin Can Make Your Job More Meaningful." *Greater Good*. The Greater Good Science Center at UC Berkeley, June 6, 2018. https://greatergood.berkeley.edu/article/item/how_oxytocin_can_make_your_job_more_meaningful.
8. Vrticka, Pascal. "Evolution of the 'Social Brain' in Humans: What Are the Benefits and Costs of Belonging to a Social Species?" *HuffPost*, November 16, 2013. https://www.huffpost.com/entry/human-social-development_b_3921942.
9. Parker, *The Art of Gathering*, 1.

10. Parker, *The Art of Gathering*, 19.

11. Parker, *The Art of Gathering*, 17.

12. Parker, *The Art of Gathering*, 17–18.

13. Allen, Courtland. "Charting Your Own Course as a Founder with Jason Fried of Basecamp." Indie Hackers, July 19, 2019. https://www.indiehackers.com/podcast/105-jason-fried-of-basecamp.

14. Basecamp. "Chapter 11: Our Rituals." *Basecamp Employee Handbook*. Accessed March 9, 2020. https://basecamp.com/handbook/11-our-rituals.

15. Basecamp, "Our Rituals."

16. Basecamp, "Our Rituals."

17. Shellenbarger, Sue. "The Power of a 'Project Beard' and Other Office Rituals." *Wall Street Journal*, June 25, 2013. https://www.wsj.com/articles/SB10001424127887323683504578567362835749272.

18. "The Most Popular TED Talks of All Time." TED Talks. Accessed March 9, 2020. https://www.ted.com/playlists/171/the_most_popular_talks_of_all.

19. Hanna, Julia. "Power Posing: Fake It Until You Make It." HBS Working Knowledge. Harvard Business School, September 20, 2010. https://hbswk.hbs.edu/item/power-posing-fake-it-until-you-make-it.

20. Gillett, Rachel. "A Fashion Designer and Founder of a $450 Million Company Explains Why She Starts Every Meeting by Ringing a Bell." *Business Insider*, November 4, 2016. https://www.businessinsider.com/eileen-fisher-starts-every-meeting-with-meditation-2016-11.

21. Keswin, Erica. Interview with Daisy Auger-Dominguez. Personal, March 9, 2020.

22. Parker, *The Art of Gathering*, 250.

23. Basecamp. "How Buffer Meets Up." The Rework Podcast, June 4, 2019. https://rework.fm/how-buffer-meets-up/.

24. Basecamp. "How Buffer Meets Up."

25. Heath, Kathryn, and Brenda F. Wensil. "To Build an Inclusive Culture, Start with Inclusive Meetings." *Harvard Business Review*, September 30, 2019. https://hbr.org/2019/09/to-build-an-inclusive-culture-start-with-inclusive-meetings.

26. Jagannathan, Meera. "Here's How to Host a Dinner Party or Meeting That's Not Completely Lame." *MarketWatch*, May 18, 2018. https://www.marketwatch.com/story/heres-how-to-host-a-dinner-party-or-meeting-thats-not-completely-lame-2018-05-18-1884855.

CHAPTER FOUR

1. Kniffin, Kevin M., Brian Wansink, Carol M. Devine, and Jeffery Sobal. "Eating Together at the Firehouse: How Workplace Commensality Relates to the Performance of Firefighters." *Human Performance* 28, no. 4 (2015): 281–306. https://doi.org/10.1080/08959285.2015.1021049.

2. Kniffin et al. "Eating Together."

3. Kniffin et al. "Eating Together."
4. Kniffin et al. "Eating Together."
5. Kniffin et al. "Eating Together."
6. Kniffin et al. "Eating Together."
7. Pentland, Alex. "The Water Cooler Effect." *Psychology Today*, November 22, 2009. https://www.psychologytoday.com/us/blog/reality-mining/200911/the-water-cooler-effect.
8. Pentland, "Water Cooler."
9. Wu, Lynn, Ben Waber, Sinan Aral, Erik Brynjolfsson, and Alex Pentland. "Mining Face-to-Face Interaction Networks Using Sociometric Badges: Predicting Productivity in an IT Configuration Task." Working paper. MIT Sloan School of Management, May 7, 2008. https://vismod.media.mit.edu/tech-reports/TR-622.pdf.
10. Kniffin et al. "Eating Together."
11. Kniffin et al. "Eating Together."
12. Kniffin et al. "Eating Together."
13. Kniffin et al. "Eating Together."
14. Kniffin et al. "Eating Together."
15. Sullivan, John. "Revealing the 'HR Professional of the Decade'— Laszlo Bock of Google." ERE Recruiting Intelligence, April 21, 2016. https://www.ere.net/revealing-the-hr-professional-of-the-decade-laszlo-bock-of-google/.
16. Fosslien, Liz. "Office Rituals and Creating Culture: 4 Habits That Make Humu." Humu, July 25, 2019. https://humu.com/2019/07/25/office-rituals-and-creating-culture-4-habits-that-make-humu-humu/.
17. McLaren, Samantha. "These 6 Companies Made Work-Life Balance More Than a Buzzword." LinkedIn Talent Blog, November 9, 2018. https://business.linkedin.com/talent-solutions/blog/hr/2018/these-companies-made-work-life-balance-more-than-a-buzzword.

CHAPTER FIVE

1. Beheshti, Naz. "New Millennial Survey Finds a 'Generation Disrupted': How Business Leaders Can Respond." *Forbes*, September 29, 2019. https://www.forbes.com/sites/nazbeheshti/2019/06/27/new-millennial-survey-finds-a-generation-disrupted-how-business-leaders-can-respond/#7a5fa09648d4.
2. Friedman, Zack. "49% Of Millennials Would Quit Their Job Within 2 Years." *Forbes*, May 22, 2019. https://www.forbes.com/sites/zackfriedman/2019/05/22/millennials-disillusioned-future/#79ee0c65353e.
3. Mejia, Zameena. "Nearly 9 out of 10 Millennials Would Consider Taking a Pay Cut to Get This." CNBC, June 28, 2018. https://www.cnbc.com/2018/06/27/nearly-9-out-of-10-millennials-would-consider-a-pay-cut-to-get-this.html.
4. Elzinga, Didier. "Is L&D More Important Than Salary?" Culture Amp Blog, July 1, 2019. https://www.cultureamp.com/blog/from-our-ceo-is-ld-more-important-than-salary/.

5. Beer, Michael, Magnus Finnström, and Derek Schrader. "Why Leadership Training Fails—and What to Do About It." *Harvard Business Review*, September 9, 2016. https://hbr.org/2016/10/why -leadership-training-fails-and-what-to-do-about-it.

6. Beer et al. "Leadership Training."

7. Beer et al. "Leadership Training."

8. McQueen, Nina. "InDay: Investing in Our Employees So They Can Invest in Themselves." LinkedIn Official Blog, July 29, 2015. https://blog.linkedin.com/2015/07/29/inday-investing-in-our -employees-so-they-can-invest-in-themselves.

9. LinkedIn. "About LinkedIn." LinkedIn Newsroom. LinkedIn Corporation. Accessed March 17, 2020. https://news.linkedin .com/about-us#statistics.

10. Akhtar, Allana. "I Toured the Surprisingly Bonkers LinkedIn Offices in the Empire State Building, Which Has a 'Speakeasy' Bar Hidden Behind a Wall of Rotary Phones. Here's What It Was Like." *Business Insider*, October 15, 2019. https://www.businessinsider .com/what-the-linkedin-offices-look-like-in-new-york-city.

11. Limeade Institute and Quantum Workplace. "2016 Well-Being & Engagement Report." Limeade Institute and Quantum Workplace, 2016. https://www.limeade.com/wp-content/uploads/2016/11 /QW-LimeadeWellBeingEngagementReport-final.pdf.

12. Nelson, Amy, Samantha Ettus, and Mindy Grossman. Other. *What's Her Story Podcast: Mindy Grossman*, October 22, 2020.

13. Strauss Einhorn, Cheryl. "How a Diverse Workforce Can Help Company Performance." *Barron's*, January 4, 2019. https:// www.barrons.com/articles/how-a-diverse-workforce-can-help -company-performance-51546625800.

CHAPTER SIX

1. Pentland, Alex. "The Water Cooler Effect." *Psychology Today*, November 22, 2009. https://www.psychologytoday.com/us/blog /reality-mining/200911/the-water-cooler-effect.

2. "Tony Schwartz." The Energy Project. Accessed March 27, 2020. https://theenergyproject.com/team/tony-schwartz/.

3. Webb, Craig. "Want More from Workers? Tell 'Em to Take a Break." Builder. Hanley Wood Media, October 4, 2016. https:// www.builderonline.com/builder-100/leadership/want-more-from -workers-tell-em-to-take-a-break_o.

4. Schwartz, Tony. "The 90-Minute Solution: Live Like a Sprinter!" *Fast Company*, July 30, 2012. https://www.fastcompany.com /1707718/90-minute-solution-live-sprinter.

5. Seiter, Courtney. "The Science of Breaks at Work." Buffer, August 23, 2017. https://open.buffer.com/science-taking-breaks-at-work/.

6. Jabr, Ferris. "Why Your Brain Needs More Downtime." *Scientific American*, October 15, 2013. https://www.scientificamerican .com/article/mental-downtime/.

7. Wigert, Ben, and Sangeeta Agrawal. "Employee Burnout, Part 1: The 5 Main Causes." Gallup, February 28, 2020. https://www

.gallup.com/workplace/237059/employee-burnout-part-main
-causes.aspx.

8. Tork. "Take Back the Lunch Break." Tork. Essity Hygiene and Health AB, May 2018. https://cdntorkprod.blob.core.windows .net/docs-c5/298/187298/original/tblb-infographic-final.pdf.

9. Tork, "Lunch Break."

10. Blankson, Amy. "4 Ways to Help Your Team Avoid Digital Distractions." *Harvard Business Review*, September 3, 2019. https://hbr.org/2019/07/4-ways-to-help-your-team-avoid-digital -distractions.

11. Moon Juice, "Our Story." Accessed March 12, 2020. https:// moonjuice.com/pages/our-story.

12. Moon Juice, "Our Story."

13. Field, Hayden. "Allbirds' San Francisco HQ Celebrates the Past But Looks to the Future." *Entrepreneur*, April 15, 2019. https:// www.entrepreneur.com/article/331257.

14. Copeland, Rob. "Trendy Sneaker Startup Allbirds Laces Up $1.4 Billion Valuation." *Wall Street Journal*, October 11, 2018. https:// www.wsj.com/articles/trendy-sneaker-startup-allbirds-laces-up -1-4-billion-valuation-1539281112.

15. Albert-Deitch, Cameron. "A Decade Ago, He Helped Lead New Zealand to the World Cup. Now, Allbirds's Founder Is Bringing Those Team-Building Lessons to His Company." *Inc.*, September 17, 2019. https://www.inc.com/cameron-albert-deitch/allbirds -tim-brown-company-culture-pro-sports.html.

16. Allbirds. "Our Story." Accessed March 12, 2020. https://www .allbirds.com/pages/our-story.

17. Channick, Robert. "Embracing March Madness: Employers Go All in with Basketball Watch Parties, Pizza and Office Pools." *Chicago Tribune*, March 23, 2019. https://www.chicagotribune .com/business/ct-biz-march-madness-offices-viewing-parties -20190318-story.html.

18. Mishkin, Shaina. "Redmond, Washington." *Money*, September 16, 2019. https://money.com/collection-post/redmond-washington/.

19. Webb, "Want More from Workers?"

20. Lange, Caroline. "From Where We Stand: Our Summer Week in Photos." Food52, September 26, 2018. https://food52.com/blog /14025-from-where-we-stand-our-summer-week-in-photos.

21. "Every Action Matters." REI Co-op. Recreational Equipment, Inc. Accessed March 23, 2020. https://www.rei.com/opt-outside.

22. Peterson, Hayley. "Why REI Closes on the Most Critical Shopping Day of the Year." *Business Insider*, November 21, 2016. https:// www.businessinsider.com/rei-closed-on-black-friday-2016-11.

23. The Black Sheep Agency. "The Black Sheep Agency." Accessed March 27, 2020. https://theblacksheepagency.com/.

CHAPTER SEVEN

1. Jenkins, Ryan. "This Is How Generation Z Employees Want Feedback." *Inc.*, June 25, 2019. https://www.inc.com/ryan-jenkins /this-is-how-generation-z-employees-want-feedback.html.
2. Cision. "Failure Drives Innovation, According to EY Survey on Gen Z." Cision PR Newswire, September 18, 2018. https:// www.prnewswire.com/news-releases/failure-drives-innovation -according-to-ey-survey-on-gen-z-300714436.html.
3. Jenkins, Ryan. "How Generation Z Will Transform the Future Workplace." *Inc.*, January 15, 2019. https://www.inc.com /ryan-jenkins/the-2019-workplace-7-ways-generation-z-will -shape-it.html.
4. Willyerd, Karie. "Millennials Want to Be Coached at Work." *Harvard Business Review*, December 6, 2017. https://hbr.org /2015/02/millennials-want-to-be-coached-at-work.
5. Stein, Joel. "Millennials: The Me Me Generation." *Time*, May 20, 2013. https://time.com/247/millennials-the-me-me-me-generation/.
6. Next Jump. https://www.jhsph.edu/research/centers-and-institutes /institute-for-health-and-productivity-studies/_docs/promoting -healthy-workplaces/NEXT%20JUMP.pdf.
7. Next Jump. "Grow Yourself and Those Around You. Every Day." Accessed March 13, 2020. https://www.nextjump.com/careers -overview/.
8. Next Jump, "2019 Avengers Ceremony." 2019. https://www .nextjump.com/avengers-2019/.
9. Fukumoto-Pasko, Jenny. "The Meaning Behind Mustache Day." Jellyvision. May 17, 2019. https://www.jellyvision.com/news -press/meaning-behind-mustache-day/.
10. Tauck. "Tauck." Accessed March 27, 2020. https://www.tauck.com/.
11. Bundlie, Kira. "Backroads Staff Ride!" Backroads Blog. November 14, 2015. https://www.backroads.com/blog/backroads-staff-ride/.
12. Bundlie, "Backroads."
13. Bundlie, "Backroads."

CHAPTER EIGHT

1. Starbucks. "Starbucks Reports Q4 and Full Year Fiscal 2019 Results." Starbucks Investor Relations, October 30, 2019. https://investor .starbucks.com/press-releases/financial-releases/press-release -details/2019/Starbucks-Reports-Q4-and-Full-Year-Fiscal-2019 -Results/default.aspx.
2. Schultz, Howard, and Joanne Gordon. *Onward: How Starbucks Fought for Its Life Without Losing Its Soul*, 23. New York, NY: Rodale, 2019.
3. Schultz and Gordon, *Onward*, 9.
4. Trujillo, Joshua. "Starbucks Origin Trip Builds a Bridge Between Partners and Rwandan Farmers." Starbucks Stories and News.

Starbucks Corporation, May 1, 2017. https://stories.starbucks .com/stories/2017/starbucks-origin-trip-rwanda-2017/.

5. Warnick, Jennifer. "AI for Humanity: How Starbucks Plans to Use Technology to Nurture the Human Spirit." Starbucks Stories and News. Starbucks Corporation, January 10, 2020. https:// stories.starbucks.com/stories/2020/how-starbucks-plans-to-use -technology-to-nurture-the-human-spirit/.

6. LaVito, Angelica. "Starbucks Is Opening a Store in China Every 15 Hours." CNBC, December 5, 2017. https://www.cnbc.com/2017 /12/05/starbucks-is-opening-a-store-in-china-every-15-hours .html.

7. McCormick Place. "Facility Overview." Accessed March 17, 2020. https://www.mccormickplace.com/facility-overview/.

CHAPTER NINE

1. Silverberg, Nicole. "To Hell and Back Again: A Day with the Marie Kondo Method." GQ, January 4, 2019. https://www.gq.com /story/marie-kondo-purge-diary.

2. Cornish, Audie, Brian Edwards, Braden Pothier, and Rachel Syme. "Thrift Stores Say They're Swamped with Donations After 'Tidying Up with Marie Kondo.'" All Things Considered. NPR, January 21, 2019. https://www.npr.org/2019/01/21/687255642 /thrift-stores-say-theyre-swamped-with-donations-after-tidying -up-with-marie-kond.

3. GoHealth Urgent Care. "About GoHealth Urgent Care." April 23, 2020. https://www.gohealthuc.com/about.

4. Abela, Peter. "Sweep the Sheds." Medium, May 28, 2019. https://medium.com/@LifeHacksLoveDad/sweep-the-sheds -eb419b06f9ea.

5. Knies, David. "'Sweep The Shed'—How Team Culture Made New Zealand a Global Superpower." Adventures in the Innovation Economy, May 23, 2017. http://dknies.com/blog/2017/3/12/sweep -the-floor-how-culture-turns-a-tiny-island-nation-into-a-global -force.

6. Alter, Alexandra. "How Marie Kondo Declutters During a Pandemic." New York Times, March 20, 2020. https://www .nytimes.com/2020/03/20/business/marie-kondo-coronavirus -diary.html.

CHAPTER TEN

1. Robinson, Bryan. "'Loneliness on the Job Is a Public Health Crisis': Former Surgeon General Reveals What This Means for You." Forbes, January 3, 2020. https://www.forbes.com /sites/bryanrobinson/2020/01/03/loneliness-on-the-job-is -a-public-health-crisis-former-surgeon-general-reveals-what-this -means-for-you/#5050b11a13d2.

POSTSCRIPT

1. Ryland, Alan. "Brookings Institution Debunks the Trump Administration's Report on the Dropping Unemployment Rate." PoliticusUSA, June 8, 2020. https://www.politicususa.com/2020/06/08/brookings-institution-debunks-the-trump-administrations-report-on-the-dropping-unemployment-rate.html.

2. Grant, Heidi. "New Research: Rituals Make Us Value Things More." *Harvard Business Review*, June 16, 2015. https://hbr.org/2013/12/new-research-rituals-make-us-value-things-more.

3. Grant, "New Research."

4. Berinato, Scott. "The Restorative Power of Ritual." *Harvard Business Review*, April 20, 2020. https://hbr.org/2020/04/the-restorative-power-of-ritual.

5. Driscoll, Mary, and Michael D. Watkins. "Onboarding a New Leader—Remotely." *Harvard Business Review*, May 18, 2020. https://hbr.org/2020/05/onboarding-a-new-leader-remotely.

6. Kelso, Alicia. "Why Chipotle Will Come Out of the Coronavirus Crisis Stronger Than Ever." *Forbes*, April 23, 2020. https://www.forbes.com/sites/aliciakelso/2020/04/23/why-chipotle-will-come-out-of-the-coronavirus-crisis-stronger-than-ever/#57bfd26e68ca.

7. Nordgren, Loran, and David Schonthal. "How to Foster Better Working Relationships Even When You're Quarantined." *Fast Company*, April 17, 2020. https://www.fastcompany.com/90491969/how-to-foster-better-working-relationships-even-when-youre-quarantined.

8. Gelles, David. "The One Ritual Keeping Me Sane During Covid-19." CNN, April 25, 2020. https://www.cnn.com/2020/04/25/opinions/covid-19-ritual-grieving-ice-cream-gelles/index.html.

INDEX

ABOUT THE AUTHOR

Erica Keswin is a bestselling author, internationally sought-after speaker, and founder of the Spaghetti Project, a roving ritual devoted to sharing the science and stories of relationships at work. She helps top of the-class businesses, organizations, and individuals improve their performance by honoring relationships in every context, always with an eye toward high-tech for human touch. Erica was named one of Marshall Goldsmith's Top 100 Coaches in 2020, as well as one of Business Insider's most innovative coaches of 2020. Her bestselling book, *Bring Your Human to Work: 10 Surefire Ways to Design a Workplace That's Good for People, Great for Business, and Just Might Change the World,* was published in 2018 by McGraw Hill.